DAVID EDDIE

HOUSEBROKEN

CONFESSIONS OF A

STAY-AT-HOME DAD

random
house
canada

Canadian Cataloguing in Publication Data

Eddie, David
  Housebroken: confessions of a stay-at-home dad

ISBN 0-679-31002-9

1. Househusbands — Ontario — Toronto.   2. Father and child.
I. Title.

HQ756.6.E32 1999   305.33'64'092   C99-931441-6

"Too Tired" by Maxwell Davis, Sam Ling and John Watson
Copyright © 1955 & 1983 Powerforce Music (BMI)
Text design: Gordon Robertson

Printed and bound in the United States of America

10 9 8 7 6 5 4 3 2 1

I'm too tired, too tired for anything.

— *Johnny "Guitar" Watson*

CONTENTS

PREFACE

"When do you write?" a lot of people ask when they find out I'm a househusband and stay-at-home dad.

Well, it's tricky and complicated. My wife, Pam, is a TV news reporter/anchor. She reports Monday to Wednesday and anchors on the weekends. She has Thursdays and Fridays off, so I work those days. On Tuesday mornings my mother, recently retired, looks after our son Nicholas (who's two as I write this). On Wednesdays our part-time nanny, Audrey, comes in for four hours, from 9:30 to 1:30.

It's a patchwork arrangement, like most people's these days. We didn't exactly plan it this way; it evolved. From chaos I have wrestled six mornings a week to write, and I'm grateful. But still, it never seems like enough. All my competition seems to be gay, single, childless or else has the wherewithal to keep their kids in deep background.

Meanwhile I'm all too aware we're paying someone eight dollars an hour, or my mother's taking time from the sweet bliss of retirement, or Pam is looking after him on her day off—all so I can noodle around in my office seeking le mot juste or flat-out procrastinating (ironing shirts, reading a magazine or novel, chatting on the phone).

I write at top speed, in a festering stew of guilt, with distraction bombs going off outside my door every few minutes like fireworks at a patriotic display. Right now, for example, Audrey's changing Nicholas's diaper not five feet from my door. He's screaming, crying and carrying on. No doubt I'll be checking the situation out very soon (I'm not sure which is more distracting, his crying or his musical laughter). In fact, excuse me, I should probably check it out *right now*.

It's nothing; he's just tired. . . . My point, gentle reader ("and still gentler purchaser!" as Byron would say), is I don't have time and anyway I'm too tired to adopt a fake persona or embroider my writing with little faux-poetic prose-doilies, as seems to be the current fashion. I want to portray life as it is and myself as a human being, warts and all, as they say. Not only warts, but dandruff, halitosis and hemorrhoids (at least I *hope* they're hemorrhoids. I haven't been able to bring myself to ask a doctor to check it out). The unvarnished, rarely vacuumed truth, in other words. With Nicholas on the scene, the urge is stronger than ever. He's going to read this someday. Am I going to lie to *him*? Allow me to quote Michel de Montaigne, the great sixteenth-century French essayist, in support of my sentiments:

> This book was written in good faith, reader. It warns you from the outset that in it I have set myself no goal

but a domestic and private one. . . . If I had written to seek the world's favor, I should have bedecked myself better, and should present myself in a studied posture. I want to be seen here in my simple, natural, ordinary fashion, without straining or artifice; for it is myself that I portray. My defects will here be read to the life, and also my natural form, as far as respect for the public has allowed.

Of course, as with all memoirs, you have to remember that memory is filtered through the imagination: the action, dialogue and internal monologue in this book are all reproduced as I *imagine* I remember them, or as I remember imagining them. Also, I've changed the names and some biographical details of some of the characters, mostly at their requests.

One obvious irony of this book is that at times I had to be a lousy househusband and bad dad in order to write it, especially towards the end. And it was only thanks to Pam's willingness to do double duty and eat lots of pizza and takeout that I could get it done at all. Without her, this book would be an anecdote and a couple of aphorisms; so it goes without saying it's dedicated to her. But I couldn't have done it without my mother, either, who came in to pinch hit more times than I can count. So: to my wife and my mother.

1. A SQUARE PEG

"You're doing a good job," the guy behind the counter at the butcher's shop says.

That's funny; it sure doesn't feel like it. Nicholas is
six months old. Pam's been back to work for a month. I'm
pretty new at this and very shaky. I've lost his pacifier
(again); he's fussing and squirming—on the verge of a
major tantrum, I can tell, complete with tomato-red face
and hot tears streaming down his cheeks—and the stroller's
blocking traffic in the long, narrow store. Though it's four
in the afternoon, he's still in his sleep-suit, same one he
wore yesterday, the front festooned with crusty food. Earlier a woman stopped me in the street and said something
over and over again in Chinese, fingering the sleeves of
his outfit.

"I'm sorry, I don't understand you. I don't understand
what you're saying," I kept telling her. But I was lying. I knew

perfectly well what she was saying. In the universal language of interfering busybodies and tsk-tsking babushkas everywhere, she was saying, "Your baby cold. Needs another layer. You bad dad. You very, very bad dad."

I feel, in fact, like I have BAD DAD tattooed on my forehead as I jam a carton of homo milk between his lips, trying to get him to drink from the spout, teenager-style. It works, sort of: he drinks greedily, hungrily, like a neglected orphan-boy, the milk coursing down his cheeks and soaking the front of his PJs.

"Thanks," I tell the butcher. "Could I have a boneless pork roast, please?"

You've probably seen us around: huge, hulking brutes, some of us, stubbled, troubled, humbled, baffled and hassled, pushing strollers down the street, shopping carts down the aisle or swings in the park. Every day there are more of us. We're househusbands; hear us roar!

I never meant to become one, of course. I don't think many young men wake up in the middle of the night thinking, "Now I know what I want to be in life! A househusband and stay-at-home dad!" But who knows? Maybe someday that will change. Obviously we're in the middle of a revolution in the workplace. A recent study by the Families and Work Institute in New York suggests that women now earn more than half the income in 45 percent of the households in the United States. If you factor in single, divorced and widowed women, you could say that women earn more than half the money in more than half the households in America. Maybe someday there will be a corollary revolution in the home, and boys will grow up dreaming of staying home to take care of the kids.

(Don't hold your breath, though. Old habits die hard: according to another study by the same organization, even in households where women are the *sole* breadwinners, they wind up doing most or all of the housework.)

Overall, I consider it the best job I've had (well, on a nice sunny day it can be the best job in the world—and I pray to a new god now, El Niño). I treat it like a job, too: my wife, Pam, is the client, and has to be pleased with the overall product; my son, Nicholas, is the boss and orders me around on a day-to-day basis. Of course, like any boss, he can be moody and dictatorial, can freak out and call me on the carpet for poor performance of my duties. However, unlike most bosses, in my experience anyway, he's also capable of radiating pure joy and happiness, of lighting up like a Christmas tree when I report for work in the morning.

And that's a key difference, I feel, between the home-based and the office-based man. Both my client and my boss love me. I never wake up in the morning anymore with my guts churning, thinking, "Argh, I have to go to work and cross swords with all those jerks again today." Christopher Lasch called home a "haven in a heartless world," and I agree.

I was never really cut out for the rat race anyway. I mean, I know nobody really is, but I always seemed to have a harder time of it than most. I'm a square peg, I guess. For me, it's never been a question of will I get fired or not, but *how long have I got?* The moment I walk through the doors of any new job, sporting a fresh shirt and fake-confident smile, an invisible hand reaches out and overturns an invisible hourglass, and my time starts running out. From day one in any new job I'm as apprehensive as an escaped convict or soldier in mufti behind enemy lines, just waiting for the horrible moment when someone does a double take and says, "Hey, wait a second! Who's that guy? He doesn't belong here!" And then I'm off and running again, searchlights sweeping the ground, dogs barking behind me. . . .

More than anything, I can't stand the politics. My aphorism here is "I like socializing with people, but not working with them." Something about work, about having to put bread and meat on the table, brings out the worst in people, I feel, and I can't stand seeing my fellow *Homo sapiens* (ha! should be *Homo buttcoveris* or *Homo stabbinzebackski* when you're talking about people at work) behaving in such a petty, narrow-minded fashion.

Sooner or later they always smell me out. They always smell the truth in the end. I don't really like to work—not what the world calls work, anyway: reporting to the same impersonal building day in, day out, seeing the same faces, performing some pointless task. (The only thing I really miss about work is the office supplies.) What is a job, anyway, but something someone pays you to do because they don't want to do it themselves? But I have my own work to do, for my own reasons—moral, personal, philosophical—and all these *jobs* do is get in the way.

Obviously, with an attitude like this I don't last too long at any given job. My longest stint in the working world was at an organization I unaffectionately call the Cosmodemonic Broadcast Corporation. I worked there full-time for two years and part-time for four years. Why such unprecedented longevity? Perhaps because the work—writing the words the anchors read over the air—was often almost interesting, occasionally nearly creative.

But it happened there like it happens everywhere. Every time I went on vacation, it seemed, when I returned someone else was sitting in my spot, looking smug and defensive, but not at all apologetic, the victor of some invisible power struggle. It was like a game of musical chairs. And when the music stopped, I was always the one left standing, holding a pink slip.

If I have to work, I prefer lousy, boring jobs, the more mindless and mechanical the better. My favourite three-word phrase to hear on day one of any new job is "It's pretty straightforward." I like jobs on which you can read or even sleep, where all they want is a warm body, where everyone says, "Hey, it's not brain surgery" a lot. And ideally there should be an outdoor element: I don't like sitting inside all day.

Which is why being a househusband is perfect for me! Either that, or one of those guys who walk around the park, stabbing garbage with spiked sticks. In fact, when I can bear to face the truth, I realize that with my love of drudgery, inability to deal with office politics, and choice of a non-earning profession, I was probably *born* to be a househusband.

I still have stress—more, I sometimes think, than the busiest business executive. But it's stress of a different kind: trying to avoid the golden arch of his pee while I'm changing his diaper; trying to force him to eat his baby goo; and generally keeping an eyeball on him at all times, making sure he doesn't grab a fork out of the dishwasher and jab it in his eye or an electrical socket, or disappear when I turn my back, never to be heard from again, like the kid in Ian McEwan's *The Child in Time* (of course it happens when the dad is looking after her, while he's shopping for groceries).

That's stress. If a busy business executive blows a meeting, he might lose a client, maybe even his job, and I'm not pooh-poohing that. But if *I* screw up—if, say, I were absent-mindedly to push Nicholas's stroller under the wheels of a semi—I don't want to think about how that would feel. Nor do I want to try to picture the scene where I break the news to Pam, her paroxysm of grief; and afterwards, the slow dissolution of our marriage as she bravely tries to forgive me, but finds that ultimately she can't. It's unthinkable, yet it happens all the time. There's a woman at the park who told Pam she lost her kid when he was two and a half. I've wanted to ask her how, but I can't bring myself to do it. She looks so sad.

"Not on my watch" is my mantra as I push Nicholas around or monitor his activities at the park. In some ways, Pam's a softie. She cries during corny movies and even commercials, especially those featuring parent-child bonding moments. But if something happened to Nicholas on my watch, I imagine her reaction being something like "Dave, since I love you and we've been through a lot together, I'll kill you quickly. If anyone else were responsible, I'd have to torture them first."

I feel the same way. If Nicholas and I are passengers in a car and the driver appears to be driving too fast or is in any way careless or reckless, I will simply say to that person, "You realize, of course, that if we get into an accident and Nicholas is killed, I'll have to crawl on my bloody stumps to where you're lying in a pool of blood and broken teeth and finish you off myself, don't you? It's sort of like a protocol we parents have." They tend to slow down after that.

Nothing special. Like millennia of women I try to protect my child from harm. May I suggest, though, that in this department I am perhaps better equipped than a woman? I'm six-foot-five, 225 pounds, and though I haven't been getting to the gym much lately, I do lift weights here in my office/dressing room. I'm built like a big, bespectacled bouncer, basically, and if you were to approach the stroller in what appeared to be a hostile or threatening manner, I would interpose my huge wine/beer/whiskey gut between you and the baby, loom large in my pointy-toed size fourteens, casting a chilly shadow across your trembling, cowering form, and say, "May I *help* you?"

So if you see me walking down the street on a sunny day, say, tanned, dressed in a Hawaiian shirt, pushing the stroller along, whistling a little tune to myself, stopping to pat the occasional dog, you might be tempted to say, "Whew, what a life. That guy's got no worries." But you'd be wrong. Behind my whistling lips and tanned features, my brain is processing, processing, calculating odds and crunching numbers on a series of possible scenarios, like a chess computer, like Deep Blue running a safety-first sub-routine: Hmmm, that eighteen-wheeler seems to be cutting the hypotenuse of the corner: pull stroller back one metre. Hmmm, that sign is hanging by an acute angle in twenty kilometres-per-hour winds: take evasive action. Hmmm, that pit bull weighs approximately sixty kilos and its owner has three visible tattoos and two piercings: elevate child to shoulder height.

(Dogs are a tough call, actually. With a single snap of their savage jaws they could kill or permanently disfigure my child. On the other hand, Nicholas likes it when they lick his face. You have to make a split-second decision as the dog, fangs bared, muscles pumping, is charging towards your child. You have to size up not only the dog, but the owner in a glance, like a customs officer.)

The other day I was pushing Nicholas through the playground at our local park when I came upon a fortyish mom sitting on a bench with a little girl who looked about three. I nodded to the mother; Nicholas stared in mute fascination at the girl.

"Are you planning to stay here in the park for long?" she asked me out of nowhere.

"I wasn't planning to," I said. "But I could."

"Would you?" she asked—and burst into tears.

"What's the matter?" I asked, sitting down next to her. I didn't put my arm around her. She was, after all, a total stranger.

She blurted out between sobs, "There was a man here with his dog, and the dog was barking at us, and it got really close to my little girl, and he wouldn't take it away. I told him to, but he wouldn't, and it kept barking and barking, and then I started yelling at him, and he was yelling at me, and then he took out his penis, and then he went away, but then he came back, and his dog was barking at us again, and I was really, really scared." She put her face in her hands.

"He took out his penis?"

"Yes, I was yelling at him to go away and he took out his penis and he was waving it at me and yelling at me and my daughter. I'm really frightened. I think he's still somewhere in the park. . . ."

"Where?"

She pointed him out to me. He was on the far side, near the street: a smallish, dark-haired man in his early twenties, with the invariable buzz cut and baseball cap, walking a big husky puppy.

I consoled her as best I could and stuck with her until her tormentor left the park. Later, though, I reflected that some punk with a husky puppy wouldn't scare me, and if he whipped out his dick I'd kick his ass. (Unless, of course, he was a genuine tough guy, in which case he'd probably wind up kicking my ass. In a fight, it's not how big you are or what sort of shape you're in but what neighbourhood you grew up in, and, unfortunately for my pugilistic skills, I grew up in strictly middle-class enclaves.)

Still, physically, I feel well suited to my profession; temperamentally, too, I like to think. I'm one of those people whose wig becomes even more tightly screwed on when all about me people are flipping theirs. That's probably part of the reason I lasted as long as I did in TV news. In crisis situations, my pulse actually goes *down*, like a serial killer's. And you need a cool head when it comes to kids. The other night, for example, Nicholas woke up bawling in the middle of the night and refused to be soothed. Our bedroom is on the third floor of our house and his nursery is on the second floor. Pam was down there trying to soothe him. She was rocking him in her arms, singing to him, talking to him, but he was inconsolable. Suddenly Pam snapped: she screamed, and I could hear her running out of the room, sobbing with heart-wrenching sobs that went "ha-ha-ha," like they were being pulled out of her.

That's when I did an action-hero tuck-and-roll out of bed, bounded down the stairs two at a time. She was standing in the hallway, tears rolling out of her eyes.

"Take it easy, Pam," I said. "You go back to bed. I'll take over here."

She didn't hesitate, just nodded gratefully and climbed the stairs. With purposeful stride, I entered the nursery and set about figuring out what was wrong. I have a rotating system of five things I try when Nicholas is crying: 1) give bottle, 2) change diaper, 3) read favourite book to, 4) sing to while rocking in arms, 5) burp. Don't forget burping, gentlemen; sometimes when you're ready to go mad, when you've tried everything and can't figure out what's wrong, it's gas.

I can't remember what the problem was on this occasion, but eventually he calmed down, and I went back to bed. I must say I felt good, competent, useful . . . even manly. Current Hollywood movies stress supercompetence in their male heroes, but what kind of competence is it? Defusing bombs, grabbing the controls of flaming jets or out-of-control city buses and guiding them to safety, shooting people between the eyes or kicking their asses in crunchy, chop-socky punch-ups. But realistically, how often does that sort of situation come up? If you confronted one of those wisecracking, pumped-up characters with a pot full of boiling water and an egg, he couldn't hard-boil it.

I'd like to make a movie about what happens after the final fade-out and credits, after the hero saves the day and gets the girl. Back at home, our well-muscled, five-foot-tall cinema hero gets his new girlfriend pregnant, then stands around uselessly, incompetently, while she does everything: gets up in the middle of the night, changes the diapers, prepares all the meals. He starts thinking: "Whew, when's the CIA going to call with a fresh assignment? I *have* to get out of here." Meanwhile, they're exhausted, they argue, the marriage turns rocky, he can't get it up. . . .

Whereas I am the new type of superhero! I'm House-Bound Man! In the nick of time, I spring into action, averting an oncoming tantrum with a well-timed cookie, deftly defusing the ticking time bomb of Nicholas's stinking, steaming diapers while my nervous sidekick (Pam) watches over my shoulder— :04, :03, :02, :01, :01, :01 ... Phew.

As I say, though, while growing up, my dreams tended to be less about diapers than about limos, mansions and hot tubs. I could see it all: *me* in a Hollywood hot tub filled with naked Vassar girls. I'd sip champagne from a silver bucket resting on the steaming flagstones as I fielded their eager questions vis-à-vis my career: "Where do you get your inspiration, Mr. Eddie? How autobiographical is your stuff? Will one of *us* be in your next book?" One of them takes notes, perhaps, for her campus paper, holding her notebook high so as not to get the pages soggy. . . .

Well, it didn't work out like that. When I met Pam, at age thirty-one, I had become a writer, but in a much more realistic way than I'd ever pictured in my teen cheese-dreams. Basically, my career was three-tiered: on weekends I worked at the local television station, writing scripts, which paid the bills, more or less; during the week, I freelanced, writing articles for various magazines and newspapers; and of course I was working on my first novel, the first instalment of a shelf-filling magnum opus d'amour-propre I hoped (and still hope) would one day cause the world to fall to its knees and acknowledge my scintillating synapses.

A talented, youngish up-and-comer, in other words— or, viewed from another angle, a bit of a handywoman's special (lots of potential, but needs lots of work, too. A good investment? Perhaps . . .). A hardcore, hard-drinking bachelor in the Charles Bukowski mould, living above a store in the middle of Kensington Market, the breadbasket of Toronto. Not very domestic: like me, my apartment was a large, loft-y bachelor, and it was quite swish when I first moved in. But I'd single-handedly de-renovated it, turned it into a dump. One friend described the decor as "early eighties crackhouse": mattress on the floor, clothes strewn everywhere, not to mention feathers and bird droppings. As a symbol of my bachelor freedom, I allowed my pet canary, Georgie, to fly around freely. I'd trained him to defecate in his cage, sort of. In the sink, an eternal tower of dirty dishes teetered and festered. Did I have roaches? *Sí, señor.* Rodents? Check. In fact, in one infamous all-time low of poor housekeeping, a mouse slipped on a slimy dish in my sink and drowned in the greasy dishwater. (I didn't notice until my friend Max came over and said from the kitchen, "Dave, do you realize there's a *dead mouse* in your sink?")

Sometimes even I had to admit my life could use a woman's touch. However, when, in the ten thousand–degree oven of adolescence, I decided I wanted to be a writer, I swore to be an eternal bachelor. "You must become an acolyte of literature, Dave," is how I put it to myself. "You have to keep your overhead low, rent don't buy, work as little as possible to stay afloat, so you can devote more of your time and energy to writing."

Above all, no kids. I agreed with Cyril Connolly, who wrote in *Enemies of Promise*, "There is no more sombre threat to good art than the pram in the hallway." True, I thought. Kids *mediocrify* you; kids use you the way a vine uses a tree, to climb into the world. Sometimes the host organism is destroyed—or simply drained of colour and denuded of interest.

Kids, I felt, were for people who had given up on *them-selves*, who'd given in: "Well, I guess *I'll* never be a great conductor or astronaut [or whatever], but perhaps some-day little Junior will wield the baton or view the moons of Jupiter from his porthole."

I was too restless and ambitious for that! I still had big plans for me! You won't catch me in the kid trap, I swore to myself, flipping weenies on the barbecue in some suburban backyard, wearing an apron that says Kiss The Cook, while jam-smeared brats dart in and out of my legs screaming "Did so! Did not!" I had to be an outsider, a punk, a lone wolf, observing society from the fringes. If any relation-ship threatened to become too serious, I'd have to break it off brutally.

2. "SHE'S PERFECT"

Easier said than done, though. The first
time I had to put my policy into effect, I was living with my
graduate-school sweetheart in a loft in Manhattan's flower/
fur/fashion/plant/restaurant-supply district, Chelsea. She
was twenty-seven and, like many women, wanted kids by
the time she was thirty-two or thirty-three. I knew in an
abstract way I might change my mind about kids someday; but I also knew if I dithered for too long and then
said, "You know what, I've decided I can't handle it after
all," she could point me out to people in the street and
say, "There goes the cad who ruined my life." And I didn't
want that.

And now I'll tell you something that will probably make
you despise me. I left her suddenly, quit my job one day
and was on a plane the next, flying back home to Toronto. I
didn't have any money, so she put my ticket on her credit

card. In other words, I borrowed her money to leave her. I never paid her back.

What a scumbag, eh? Coward? Cad? [Insert your own insulting epithet here]? You may have a point, but have you ever tried to leave when you live with someone? It isn't easy. You have to do it suddenly, like when you take off a bandage, spraying lies, like a scared squid—or else you'll never do it. If I'd stuck around to explain, apologize, temporize, I'd still be there, and I don't think that would've been a good idea for either of us. I loved her, but perhaps not in quite the right way, and I left for the best of reasons: to spare her a lifetime of my ambivalence. She's since met and married a man named Bob, by all accounts a decent, hard-working, honest man—a man better than I in every way, in other words—and although she doesn't speak to me anymore, I've heard through the grapevine that she's had a daughter. Congratulations!

Back here, back in Toronto, I dated a series of—well, in a former era one might have called them bimbos, but since this is the tolerant, euphemistic nineties, let's call them *sexually forthright, non-rocket-scientific young women.*

Even that sounds a tad harsh. They were all wonderful women, full of vim, brio and joie de vivre, just . . . not right for me. And why would they be? Relationships begun with a drunken lunge, continued in a haze of lust and self-reproach for usually about six months. I've dubbed this era of my life "Bachelor Hell," though I have to admit I seemed to be having fun at the time.

The last one—my last girlfriend, the last one I didn't marry—was the one who broke me, though, who snapped my resolve to remain an eternal bachelor like the dry twig it probably was. I've dubbed her "The Princess" because of her imperious beauty and breathtaking rudeness to everyone we came into contact with: shopkeepers, waiters, waitresses, my friends. She treated everyone like serfs, slaves, vassals, her personal attendants and handmaids. Haughtily she chewed them out, before turning on her well-shod heel—"C'mon, Dave"—and storming out.

And I followed, what else? The Princess was the kind of woman who wouldn't even look at me in high school. Finally, she dumped me, via airmail from Europe, where she was checking out the latest collections for a fashion magazine. In her childish scrawl, which was so big the whole page was taken up by about eight lines, she informed me it was over and "PS I recommend the new album by Lloyd Cole and the Commotions for your summer listening."

Standing in the middle of my apartment, with the overflowing ashtrays and boxer shorts hanging off the lamp, still in my pyjamas at three in the afternoon on a weekday, reading her letter and smoking a cigarette, I thought, *I've got to make some changes*. I was like the "before" guy in an infomercial: "I used to live in a dump, ladies and gentlemen. I worked two days a week, and women dumped me without even bothering to explain why. Then I discovered these tapes!"

First I did a thorough spring cleaning of my apartment, which surprised me with all its nasty nooks and grimy crannies. With a firm hand, I cleared out all the trash, disposed of all inessential knick-knacks and bric-a-brac, scrubbed and washed. I performed a thorough cull of my wardrobe, got rid of all the rare-wears and non-starters. I even tossed out my soggy, sagging double bed, put it out on the street with a sign saying Free (I lived in a poor neighbourhood; it was gone in an hour), and bought an old army cot.

I'm going to enter a period of study and reflection, I said to myself. I'm going to become an urban hermit, live simply and religiously. Above all, no more women. With this cot I embrace the single life.

But fate doesn't respect resolutions. That's exactly when Pam came along.

Pam and I met at a launch party for my friend Doug's first novel. Well, that's not quite true. We'd met once before, Pam and I, fourteen years earlier, when my high school visited her high school for a model United Nations. I was seventeen, Pam only fourteen—but what a fourteen-year-old, gentlemen! A woman already, not only a woman, but a goddess: tall, supple yet voluptuous, a gymnast, with a long, arching neck and the features of a graceful greyhound.

The model United Nations was a gathering of all the top debate weenies from all the high schools in the area; everyone gathered in the gymnasium, sat at long rows of tables, pretended to be various countries, and debated matters of international policy. What I, the "legendary" David Eddie—stoner, streaker, class clown, petty thief and long-haired hippie freak—was doing there, I have no idea. No doubt my silver-tongued best friend Max had talked me into it, and no doubt he was in it for the girls. He was in *everything* for the girls: film club, poetry club, drama club. He was a veritable whirlwind of extracurricular activities, driven by his all-day adolescent boner to rise above his natural sloth. (Meanwhile, *my* all-day boner told me, "Do whatever Max says.") Obviously, he must have been involved in debating, too, though I don't remember ever seeing him in a formal debate before or since.

Max and I were some tiny African country. I can't remember which one. Cameroon? Togo? Sierra Leone? I don't know. We didn't know much about our country back then, either. All we knew was to keep our eyes glued to John Dobson, leader of the United States and therefore the free world; whichever way he voted, we voted too. Poky little countries like ours didn't contradict the United States. If they did, they'd better be prepared to explain themselves to a high-school gym-ful of pocket-protector Poindexters and Encyclopedia Browns, some of whom even carried around little file drawers full of three-by-five-inch index cards on which they had printed all sorts of historical and geopolitical facts, ready to be whipped out to trump whatever vague "philosophical" generalities Max or I might venture to make.

Pam and her best friend Julie were Ireland. From its spot in the back of the gym, tiny Sierra Leone (or whatever) admired the lush yet forbidding beauty of Ireland, but could think of no pretext on which to suggest an alliance. Our chance came when, to the astonishment of the assembled debate weenies, Ireland voted against the United States on a point of order (something about the order in which the resolutions should be debated). Rebellious Ireland! But a rebel without a cause, as it turned out. . . .

John Dobson sprang to his feet. "Mr. Speaker! Mr. Speaker!" he cried out. "Mr. Speaker" was in fact my good friend Paul, fellow long-haired hippie (now a lawyer and considerably less hirsute) and brother to Doug, future novelist and instrument of fate. "Would Ireland care to explain its last vote?" Dobson thundered. Ireland did not. Ireland remained silent, slumped low and turned crimson.

"Perhaps Ireland would like to revise its vote?" Dobson inquired sarcastically.

"Would Ireland like to revise its vote?" Mr. Speaker repeated.

Ireland, eyes nearly table-level now, nodded.

At the end of the day's session, wily Cameroon (or whatever) timed its exit from the gym to coincide with Ireland's.

"That was bogus, how you got singled out like that," Max said.

"Yeah," I said, or something equally brilliant. I could barely bring myself to stare into the beauty-rays of my goddess, let alone speak into her nimbus. But the four of us became fast friends, smoked cigarettes and pot together, talking and standing in a huddle, and later went drinking. The evening ended, if I recall correctly, with Max sleeping in a ditch. We bonded, in other words, in the intense way only adolescents can.

I didn't see Pam again until the fateful book launch.

She was looking better than ever. Tall, elegant, yet somehow feral, with her hair slicked back she looked like some kind of prowling, predatory jungle cat. If I may quote from a (somewhat overheated) diary entry of the period: "Her pedestrian name doesn't suit her at all. Her name should be something hyphenated, should hint at her mythical stature and Amazon-like goddessness, she should be called Pam-Ra. Pam-Ra of the North . . ."

I sidled up to where she was standing, next to the canapés and crudités, grabbed my chin between thumb and forefinger and said, "Hey, Pam, does this face ring a bell?"

("A terrible opening line," Max said to me recently, "boring and clichéd." To which I merely gestured mutely around our house, the toys strewn everywhere, and the stroller against the wall.)

"Of course it does, Dave," she responded coolly.

Didn't look like I had much of a chance with her that night, though. True, we chatted amiably. We did the bump on the dance floor, and she even put her arm around me at one point. But later, when we were all standing around the kitchen, I started in on an anecdote, and Pam abruptly stalked out of the room. *That* seemed like a bad sign. I mean, usually, if you're interested in someone, you don't leave the room mid-anecdote. (Later she told me the presence of so many writers in the room had intimidated her.)

The following week, though, I held another, more private party in honour of Doug's debut. Quite a successful party, if I say so myself. It was one of those parties where everywhere you looked everyone was engaged in animated conversation and seemed extremely happy to know, or get to know, each other. My friend Nicki made a delicious punch with rum and, I think, tequila, and everything seemed to tick along smoothly (although I heard later that a couple of people got a little freaked out when they spotted the beady eyes of a mouse in the dark depths of a cupboard).

It was a weeknight, a "school night," so around midnight, people started putting on their coats and leaving in batches. Pam made as if to leave with the last batch, started putting on her coat. I came over to where she was standing and said, "*Et tu*, Pam?"

"Well, I could stick around a while, if you like," she said shyly.

A bold move, people, and one that not only changed the course of both our lives, but also led directly to the introduction of a third life into the world. (Whether it would lead to any further increases in the earth's population was a matter that required negotiation.) If Pam hadn't stuck her neck out like that, I don't think we'd be together now. In the face of what appeared to be her unwavering indifference, I was about ready to pack it in.

We chatted late into the night. Not only gorgeous and voluptuous, she was, it turned out, that rarest of creatures: a thoughtful, soulful television news reporter. She didn't even seem to mind when, after a while, I ran out of cigarettes and started smoking butts out of the ashtray. She saw the type of character I was and seemed to like me despite it, or even because of it. I could be myself in her presence; but her presence also made me better, bolder, nobler, more virtuous. This, I've noticed over the years, is the effect the best women have on me. I become my best self in their presence.

Having said that, though, I will also say this: all the conflicts—or perhaps I should say *complementary aspects*—of our characters were evident in embryo in our conversation that night.

"What do you want to do with your life?" she asked me at one point.

"I'm lucky," I answered. "I've known what I want to do since I was fourteen: write. My only problem is it's taking so long. I thought I'd be famous by the time I was twenty-four at the latest."

"You'll get there," she said (already shouldering the burden, you see, already starting to support me).

"What about you?" I asked her. "What do you want to be when you grow up? Or do you want to stay a reporter?"

"I don't know," she said, looking a little troubled. "I like my job, but . . . I don't know. I don't know if I want to do it for the rest of my life or not."

"Put it this way: you're on your deathbed, everyone's crowded around you, and they ask, 'So, Pam, did you enjoy your life? Are you glad it turned out the way it did?' And you say, 'Well, life had its ups and downs, certainly, but at least I'm glad I did blank.' How would you fill in the blank? That's what you should do."

All part of my standard shtick for people who can't make up their minds about which career to pursue. But still she couldn't answer. I ran out of butts. I had smoked them all, and we went to the corner store together to buy cigarettes. She thought about my question all the way there and all the way back. Finally, back at my apartment, sitting on the couch, she said, "Well, there is one thing I've always wanted out of life."

"What's that?"

"To have children."

It figured. The one decent woman to cross my path in years and she was a ticking biological time bomb, set to detonate my hopes of ever becoming a real writer.

But who can hold out against true love? That night, as Pam was getting into her car, a little white putt-putt Suzuki Swift, I leaned over the top of the door and gave her a kiss—a kiss that lasted until dawn, ladies and gentlemen—and although I kept begging her to come up to my apartment, she said no every time. The birds were chirping and my street, Augusta Avenue, was flooded with daylight when she finally sparked up the four-cylinder engine of her little sewing machine and tootled off.

The next time I saw her, unfortunately, was two days later at the memorial service for an old high-school acquaintance who had shot herself for reasons unknown to me. Pam picked me up at my apartment and drove me to the service. In the car, she acted cool, made no reference to our three-hour kiss, just drove and made small talk, like it never happened.

"Listen, Pam, I have to ask," I said finally, slumped down in the passenger seat. "Do you have any thoughts or feelings about the other night?"

"Well, I was a bit drunk. I don't think it would have happened otherwise," she said with a laugh, plunging me into a dank pit of despair.

After the memorial service, we stood around on the lawn, talking, smoking and sipping white wine. Pam, Julie and I hopped into her car and we all drove back to my place.

"Anyone like to come up for a drink?"

"I don't think so," Pam said. "I have to get up early for work."

"I'd like to come up," Julie said.

Pam drove off. Up in my apartment, I poured Julie a glass of red wine and one for myself. I sat on the chair. She sat on the edge of the bed.

"You like Pam, don't you?" she asked in her usual forthright way.

"I do," I said, with equal candour.

"I don't blame you. If I were a man, I'd want to date her. I'd be all over her! She's *perfect*."

I smiled, and sipped my wine. Like me, Julie is capable of expressing herself in dramatic terms at times.

"What do you mean *perfect*, Julie? Everyone has faults," I said.

"*She* doesn't. I've known her for fourteen years, and I'm telling you, she doesn't have any faults!"

Now that's loyalty, I thought. I wished *my* friends would go around telling people how perfect I was; but I knew it was quite the opposite. They love to exhume all the skeletons from my closet and rattle them in a new girlfriend's face. ("I couldn't believe how many people, when we first started seeing each other, took me aside to tell me stories about your past," Pam says now.)

"If she has anything you could call a flaw," Julie said, after a pause, "it's that she's too picky when it comes to men."

"What do you mean?"

"She's been single for *five years*. Think about it. All you have to do is look at her to know it's not for lack of offers."

". . . yeah."

"Oh, she'll date guys—she'll go on *one date*. But they always blow it somehow. They try to act too blasé, or they come on too strong, or they say the wrong thing. They make one mistake and—pffft!—they're toast."

"What would you do in my shoes?"

Julie frowned thoughtfully, sipping her wine.

"Pam likes you. She thinks you're funny," she said finally. "You may have a chance. Ask her out on a date. But don't be too blasé. On the other hand, don't come on all hot and heavy, either. You have to show her you're interested, but meanwhile preserve an aura of mystery."

That night, drifting off to sleep, I had a mental image of myself crossing a rickety wooden bridge that stretched across a chasm, the chasm that separates people from one another. Suddenly a little troll appeared out of nowhere and asked an enigmatic question. If I got it right, I could cross to the other side; if not, I would plummet to my death: "What walks on four legs in the morning, two legs in the afternoon and three legs in the evening?"

"A dog that joins the circus then gets hit by a truck?— AIEEEEE!"

The next morning, after eating, out of nervousness, three bananas, I called Pam. Julie said Pam thought I was funny, so I made with the jokes. I was like a Borscht Belt comic from Hell's Poconos: Hey ladies and germs, I just flew in from Chicago, and, boy, are my arms tired (badump-ching!). But seriously, folks, my hotel room was so small I had to go into the hall to change my mind (badump-ching!). When I put the key in the lock, I broke the window (badump-ching!). Coolly Pam parried my thrusts and finally agreed to a date that Friday.

The date went well. I should write a pamphlet describing that date for the Eddie-fication of bachelors everywhere. "Halfway through our first date, I was already in love with Dave," Pam tells people now. Little did she realize what evil scheming and Machiavellian machinations went on behind the scenes to lead her to that deceptively simple conclusion.

Like all great works of art, the date was a combination of talent, painstaking labour and serendipity. "Genius is the infinite capacity for taking pains," someone said, and I took great pains. First, I invited her over to my house for drinks and snacks. The reason for this, gentlemen, was threefold: 1) she'd already have set foot in my house at the beginning of the evening, so it wouldn't be such a big deal to cross the threshold later on; 2) we'd both loosen up a bit before dinner and could order laconically at the restaurant because we wouldn't be distracted by extreme hunger or thirst; 3) I would be the host, both symbolically and in reality—I would choose the music, lighting, atmosphere and the snacks and drinks.

I laid on a carefully selected spread with not one, but two bottles of wine. My formula for buying wine is to look for four words on the label: *appellation Bordeaux supérieure contrôlée*. The *supérieure* is extremely important. I've been disappointed by a Bordeaux, but never by a Bordeaux *supérieure*. Also various snacks: pâtés, breads, cold meats, artichokes and salmon mousse, all carefully laid out on my trunk/coffee table. And candles everywhere.

"Oh, look!" she said, spotting the salmon-and-spinach mousse on my trunk/coffee table. "My favourite! How did you know?" This was the serendipity element, boys.

After the snacks, we headed to Vanipha, a great Thai and Laotian restaurant just down the street. Again, all a part of my sinister plan. I chose a restaurant near my apartment so there would be no unromantic driving hassles on our first date, and so it wouldn't be a big deal to retire to my apartment after dinner.

Halfway through dinner, Pam shyly reached across the table for my hand; later, we kissed; and I hope it is not ungentlemanly to say that that night she did not refuse to come up to my apartment. The rest is history.

(But it was a close call. Months later, Pam told me she had had a pre-arranged blind date with a balding environmentalist the night after our first date(!). Not only that, she went on the date (!!), because she didn't want to cancel. Moreover, she liked him, and she *was* getting tired of being single for five years. She says now, with a sly smile, that she probably would have settled for the environmentalist if I hadn't come along first. Poor environmentalist! He missed out by *one night*. I hope things worked out for him and he found someone else and happiness. Here's mud in your eye!)

The reason I mention all this is because it's important. "He who weds a good wife, it is as if he has fulfilled all the precepts of the Torah," as the Talmud reminds us.

Easy for you to say, Mr. Smug, you may be thinking. You found your Mrs. Right. What about the rest of us? You have no idea what it's like out here, it's a nightmare, impossible to meet anyone decent, etc. Well, I have three words of advice for all you bachelors and bachelorettes who aspire to coupledom (and I realize there are some who don't): mingle, mingle, mingle. I feel so strongly about this point, I've even made up a little jingle about it. It doesn't really have a tune; you're supposed to belt it out like a tragic diva on her way down after an iffy career in the first place:

When you're single,
You've *got* to mingle,
Hang out your shingle
Don't be Kris Kringle!

The last line is a bit of a stretch, I admit. It's a reference to staying holed up by yourself, like Kris Kringle at the North Pole. But you see my point. Even if you're just going out with friends or people from work, people you're not even attracted to or interested in, mingle, mingle, mingle. You never know, one of them might have a brother or sister, or friend. I can't believe people who sit home night after night and then complain they can't meet anyone. Look at me: I went out pretty much every night from age fifteen to thirty-one before I met Pam. I turned nothing down except my collar. I would have gone to the opening of a mailbox if there were snacks and drinks and mingling involved. I mean, it's not like it's that painful a chore to go out all the time, and the side benefit was I finally met Pam.

I'm glad I went out so much when I had the chance, too, because having a kid puts the kibosh on all that. *Now* I see why TV's so popular. You're exhausted, emotionally drained, too tired to talk, pinned to the house with your spouse—what else are you going to do? It would be too weird just to sit around the living room together reading, though I'm trying to figure out a way. Recently I was talking on the phone, long-distance, to Julie—she lives in Vancouver now—and she told me that she and her boyfriend crawl into bed right after dinner and read. That might be an idea. Maybe I'll suggest it to Pam.

But that's now, and I was talking about then. Two weeks after our first date, we went to Max's cottage. The night we arrived, we stayed up late, drinking and talking. The next morning I was getting up, putting on my pants. Pam was in bed, leaning on one elbow, watching me and having, as I recall, an eye-opener beer, when suddenly she blurted out, as if without thinking, "I love you."

"I love you, too," I blurted back, and realized that, for the first time in three years, it was actually true.

3. A CAD'S FEAR

OF KIDS

Anyway, the whole question of having kids seemed like a long way off. Pam was twenty-eight and, like many women—like my ex-grad-school-sweetheart—wanted kids by the time she was thirty-three. (The chance of having a child with birth defects, like Down's syndrome, rises sharply if you have a kid after that.) Plenty of time, I figured, to contemplate the problem from various angles, maybe come up with some sort of compromise—a nice, fluffy puppy maybe?

But time munches on, gnashing our lives between its masticating mandibles, gobbling up days, wolfing down weeks, choking back years. As one of my ex-girlfriends' mothers used to say, "You blink, and you're thirty; cough, and you're forty; sneeze, and you're fifty."

I blinked, and Pam was thirty, fists on hips, saying to me, "Either agree *now* to fertilize my ovaries within the next three years, or pack your bags." Why now? Because if I said no, she needed the next three years to find another suitable donor—oops, I mean *suitor*—and get him to the point where he was ready to shoulder the burden of fatherhood.

I wasn't offended; I understood. Something happens to women in their late twenties and early thirties. Mother Nature takes them over, like a benign Beelzebub, starts to speak to them and through them.

"It is time," she whispers in their ears. "He'll have to do. Tonight, bury your diaphragm in the backyard, by the light of a harvest moon, which I shall provide, and make all his drinks doubles. If he still says no, you must find another."

A terrible, terrible decision. I loved her and I wanted what she wanted; but I never wanted kids. To write, I'd found, you needed two things: 1) time, 2) to be well-rested. You can drag yourself to a job in almost any condition (as I've demonstrated on numerous occasions), but writing's a bit like chess: you need to be in half-decent shape in order to compete at the highest levels. Both of these preconditions went out the window, it seemed, when you had kids.

Then there's the external pressure to switch to another, more lucrative profession. It's all very well to pursue your adolescent dream of being a starving writer into your thirties, as long as you're childless. The world tends to view it as cute, quaint, part of your quixotic charm. When you have a kid, though, that all changes. Suddenly you're selfish, irresponsible, a cad, a knave: "Did you hear? Dave's having a kid and he's still working on his 'Great Novel.'"

"Oh, what a jerk!"

And parenthood always looked like a nightmare to me from the outside. You're harried, hassled, get no sleep, spend all your money, can't go out—can't even *pop out*, it seemed; you have to get a babysitter just to have a cup of coffee with someone. You're starved for adult society; all day long you have to pretend to be interested in comments like "Look, Dad! All the buttons on my shirt are in a row." Let's face it, I said to myself, we don't bring them into the world for their conversation: ten years of stating the obvious, followed by ten years of sullen silence, then a lifetime of cash requests.

Of course, every time you ask harried, frazzled, at-the-point-of-snapping parents, "Was it worth it? Are you happy you did it? Would you do it over again?" they always say, "Oh, yes. It's wonderful. Wait until you have your own, Dave, you'll see." But I was always afraid that once I'd taken the plunge, they'd rip off their (metaphorical) rubber masks and say, "Ha! Got you! We lied! Welcome to Kiddie Hell, Dave, a never-ending, non-stop roller coaster of sheer torture! It's sort of like Disneyland, except you can *never leave*."

"But you said—"

"Yes, well, sorry about that, Dave. It was the only way we could get you to take that fatal, irrevocable step. It's a little pact we parents have. We hold secret meetings on Saturday mornings when all those lucky bachelors are still asleep. If it's any consolation, you can get your revenge on the next naive bachelor who asks *your* advice."

People will tell you parenthood's great. But then people say all kinds of crazy things, like Buffalo is a great place to visit; accounting is actually an interesting, rewarding profession; and liver is delicious if prepared a certain way.

"Kids love you unconditionally." You hear this a lot, too. But listen: I *remember* being a kid. My parents were benign blobs in vaguely human shape who either bestowed or withheld candy, toys and other treats. If they gave me a piece of candy I felt *gratification*, which is very different from gratitude. Kids need to be taught gratitude, and I remember the day I learned it. I was maybe seven, and we'd stayed at my parents' friends' place for a week. "Bye," I said over my shoulder when it was time to go. Outside, my mother grabbed me by the shoulder and told me they'd just put me up for a week, worked hard to make me happy, and now I was going to march back in there and thank them. I did, and as I was thanking them I felt the vague stirring, for the first time in my life, of something resembling actual gratitude. Which is why teaching your kid manners is so important. External actions create internal civility.

But unconditional love? I don't remember feeling any of that. Maybe I began to love my parents at around age thirty. . . .

I checked the bios of my favourite boho/ghetto literary heroes, to see how they handled the day-to-day realities of child-rearing. The short answer is: not well. The somewhat longer answer is: really not very well at all. Henry Miller, for example, loved his two children Val and Tony very much. However, when he actually had to look after them for a couple of weeks, they nearly broke him—and he had the help of a friend, Winslow Homer, who could cook. During those two weeks, Miller couldn't write, couldn't even return correspondence. His description of those two weeks, in *Big Sur and the Oranges of Hieronymus Bosch*, is far more hair-raising than the tales of penury and promiscuity in his earlier work, because he deals with an actual issue: art versus family: "To devote a whole morning to a three-year-old boy full of piss and vinegar is a job for someone with six hands and three pairs of legs. No matter what we decided to play, the jig lasted only a few minutes. Every toy in the place had been taken out, used, and thrown aside in less than an hour."

Miller keeps praying for a nanny to magically appear, to float down to his Big Sur compound with an umbrella like Mary Poppins: "In my dreams I always pictured my savior in the guise of a Hindu, Javanese or Mexican, a woman of the people, simple, not too intelligent, but definitely possessed of that one great prerequisite: *patience*." No such entity arrived, and eventually Miller had to hand off his kids to their mother, Lepska.

Likewise, Charles Bukowski was proud at the hospital when his girlfriend, Frances, gave birth to Marina Louise Bukowski. But when they got home, it was a different story. According to *Hank*, his biography: "With two people sharing his life twenty-four hours a day, he began to feel crowded. Frances had diapers to wash and both of their own clothes to clean, although Hank mainly sent his shirts to a Chinese laundry (laundry became a major bone of contention between them)." Eventually, Frances goes to visit her other children, taking Marina with her. "Hank took them to the bus station, said good-bye, and went back to his routine. Both of them knew that when Frances returned their living arrangement would have to change." End of chapter, end of relationship, pretty much: she never comes back to live with him.

Well, you might say, Bukowski and Miller aren't exactly what you'd call family men. But neither was I! Growing up, I did whatever I could to avoid my family, seeking out friends, strangers, lovers, anyone with DNA different from my own. Nothing was wrong with my family, just all that consanguinity in the air gave me the willies. As soon as I was old enough, I lit out, seeking adventure (although I also returned to the bosom of my family several times for a variety of reasons, all financial).

So who was I to take on the sacred mantle of parenthood? I'd never even been much good with plants or pets. If friends asked me to water their plants while they went on vacation, they invariably returned to withered stumps and dried-out stalks. As an adult, I'd had three pets: a canary and two finches. The canary, Georgie, died by misadventure. I was chasing him around my apartment, drunk, trying to impress a potential girlfriend with how tame he was, when he flew behind the bookcase and was squished. One of the finches committed suicide. I came home and found it feet-up in the bottom of its cage with its feed bucket over its face. I cold-bloodedly *murdered* the other one, set it free from my balcony to try its luck on the mean streets of the city. (Sometimes, to assuage my guilt, I imagine it fell in with a friendly gang of pigeons and is still alive, living off handouts in the park, happy to be free; at other times, though, I picture it flapping cold and wet in the gutter before a rat drags it off to his sewer torture-chamber.) Why did I murder that poor helpless finch? Because finches make this unk-unk, unk-unk sound all day long, even when you put a cloth over the cage. It was driving me crazy.

So what kind of dad would I make?

"You'd make a great dad, Dave," Mother Nature said, using Pam as her ventriloquist's dummy. "And you'll still be able to write, probably better than ever."

Hmmm . . . I had noticed that over the two-year course of our relationship, Pam was almost always right in matters of substance and practicality—and in all other matters, too. And I say "almost always right" simply for the sake of verisimilitude. In truth I can't seem to recall a single occasion when I was right and she was wrong. I might have seemed to be right; I might even have won the argument, ticking off logical points on my fingers and finally forcing Pam to apologize for her outrageous behaviour. But when the smoke cleared and the dust settled, it would always turn out that Pam had been right all along.

The discovery of my essential erroneousness, my fundamental flawfulness, by the way, was a crucial step in my personal path to wisdom. I never chew anyone out anymore. I know, for example, that if I rant and rave at the clerk in the photofinishing shop, demand to see the manager, in the end it will turn out that I had my thumb on the lens. I think that's why I like church so much—on the rare occasions I go. Sitting in a darkened room, begging for forgiveness, getting on your knees and saying, "Good Lord, I've been a jerk all week long, and I have absolutely no excuse. All I can do is pray for Your forgiveness." I don't know, it just feels right to me.

Perhaps "essential erroneousness" isn't the best way to put it. Perhaps a better way to put it is: it's important to know what your department in this life is, and what is not. That's my fervent prayer these days: "Lord, grant me the wisdom to know what is and what is not my department, and when something isn't my department, the serenity to turn it over to my handlers." Pam's departments were housing, transportation, taxes, travel and babies. Mine were writing and miscellaneous. Making sure we never ran out of coffee. Ummm . . . oh, yes, of course: cooking and all social arrangements, including the almost completely single-handed planning and execution of dinner parties. But babies were clearly not my department; whereas Pam was obviously not only a baby *handler*, but a baby *wrangler* (the highest designation).

I didn't want to return to the crackling flames of Bachelor Hell, the fire that burneth but consumeth not. I had a feeling that this time it would be a one-way ticket, and I didn't want to wind up cruising the clubs at, say, forty-five, trying to pick up "chicks" with my outdated lingo:

"Hey, baby, what's coming down the track?"

"Buzz off, pops!"

I had been starting to think, though, that perhaps if I wanted fun, available, wild and crazy friends to hang out with all the time, I'd have to create them myself, like Dr. Frankenstein. My ideal of friendship prevailed in my sophomore year of college, when I was twenty and fifteen of us lived in an A-frame house on the edge of campus. Men and women alike, we lay all over each other in our nightclothes in the living room, in front of a fire, knocked on each others' doors late at night for advice. Those were the days. I remember once taking a shower and my friend Andrew ripping open the shower curtain, saying, "Come on, Dave, let's go play!"

But when you hit your thirties, everyone becomes so damnably busy. One day, I bumped into an old high-school acquaintance, Suzy, outside the library. (Actually, she and I were more than mere acquaintances, we'd gone to the junior prom together. "What's it like going out with a *giant*?" all her friends asked her. I was freakishly tall in high school; I still am now, for that matter.)

"Suzy! What's happening?" I asked her.

"Dave! Great to see you!"

After we chatted a while, she said, "We should get together sometime and have a cup of coffee."

"Sure, Suze," I said. "When?"

"Well, I'm pretty busy right now," she said, frowning and thinking. "How about sometime in February?"

This was in early *October*.

Kids re-introduce the element of chaos into your life. One day Pam and I went to her sister's for dinner. Pam's sister has three kids: Sam, Nate and Max. It was a warm summer night and, before dinner, we sat on the porch and chatted. Suddenly Nate, who was three at the time, jumped into my lap, buck-naked, wriggling like a fish and grinning crazily.

I need more of this sort of thing in my life, I thought. I need more madness, chaos and wildness.

Max has made the point that if you don't have kids, you run the risk of becoming too fastidious, of getting too into your apartment or your dog or your car. One married guy I know had a vasectomy so he could never have a kid, for all the reasons listed above. But now he's a little *tetched* on the subject of his sports car, a Porsche. He has a photo album full of pictures of it, and on weekends he even takes it to a little track on the outskirts of town where he races it against other middle-aged guys who are also crazy about their cars. A tragic misuse of time and energy, if not talent.

It *would* be kind of fun to have a little sidekick, a pint-sized version of me who would blurt out ultra-candid comments to imperfect strangers on the subway, like "Wow, mister, you sure have knobbly knees." (I, of course, would pretend to rebuke him, then later pat him on the head and give him a chocolate, saying, "Good work, kid. Keep it up.")

Somehow it was this last image that persuaded me. I quashed my qualms and agreed to Pam's terms—or, rather, to a compromise. She wanted two children, I didn't want any, so we agreed on "one—and we'll see." Two, and you're a referee; three, you play zone, as a friend of mine says. But one I thought I could maybe handle. If not, well, I'd be in trouble.

I only had one counter-demand, which I tried to put to Pam as pleasantly as possible (Pam grew up in the suburbs and has many happy memories, so I had to choose my words carefully). "All I ask, Pam, is that you don't drag me to the suburbs. I'm a city person. I'd wither and die out there, Pam. I mean, no offence to anyone who lives in the suburbs or grew up there, but it's always seemed like a living death to me. You have to get in your car to buy a pack of cigarettes or a carton of milk. That'd kill me, Pam. The suburbs would just about finish me off," I concluded dramatically.

"*Please*, Dave," Pam responded frostily. "I don't want to go to the suburbs any more than you do. Whatever gave you that idea?"

I had a feeling my vacillations were all pretty much moot, anyway. I was like a fly in a Venus flytrap. "Well, it's been nice knowing you," the fly says to the Venus flytrap. "Seriously, we should keep in touch. However—bzzzt, bzzzt, hmph, that's funny, I seem to be stuck—I'm just not ready for a commitment right now, but—bzzzt, bzzzt, damn, that's strange, I can't move my leg—anyway, I'll give you a call as soon as I can."

Munch, munch, the Venus flytrap responds. . . .

Pam's "nesting instinct" kicked in, and she started looking around for a house. Her granny laid twenty grand on her, or else we never would have been able to consider it. And with Pam's solid salary and spotless credit history, she was easily able to obtain a "pre-approved mortgage." In other words, if she saw a house she liked, all she had to do was say, "I want it," and the house was hers (in thirty or forty years). I, who have never been approved, let alone pre-approved for anything, was impressed. Naturally my name, the name of an international credit felon (I never did pay back my student loans), appeared nowhere on the papers. I was kept deep in the background, a shadowy, tenant-like figure who would move in after she bought the house—like when a car pulls over for a sexy hitchhiker and her boyfriend comes running out of the bushes.

I experience a shudder of shame whenever I recall my role in the house-hunting process. Thanks in part to my execrable two-day-a-week earnings, our price ceiling was pretty much the bottom of the market. We looked at a lot of dumps. I remember once, after we looked at a particularly depressing potential domicile, a low-slung two-storey in a row of houses all exactly the same on a depressing little side street, saying to Pam as we drove off, "You know, Pam, sometimes I think you've got the wrong guy. I feel like you have this whole picture of how your life is going to be, with the house and the kids and the dog, and you're trying to fit me in the blank spot marked husband. But I don't fit. I'm not that kind of guy. I *like* to rent; sometimes I think I was born to rent. I like keeping my overhead low, so I have to do fewer stupid jobs to earn a living. I like having a manageable monthly nut that's always the same, with no surprises. When you rent and there's a problem, it's not your problem, it's the landlord's problem. You just phone him up and say, 'My fucking faucet's dripping,' and go back to whatever you were doing. I like that. I like the lack of responsibility—you know what I'm saying? Ownership dulls your wits: you're thinking about termites and your furnace all the time, and you have no time to think about anything else."

I warmed to my topic and, cheeks glowing, delivered what I considered to be an inspired lecture on the rewards of renting versus the onerousness of ownership. Did not the greatest philosophers of antiquity keep their possessions to a minimum? My favourite philosopher, Diogenes the Cynic, "Socrates gone mad," slept on his cloak and carried all his possessions around in a small leather wallet. When Alexander the Great, the most powerful conqueror and ruler in history, came over to where the flat-broke Diogenes was sitting and asked if there was anything he could do to help him, Diogenes said, "Yes. Get out of my sunlight."

I love that kind of thing! And incorporated it into my lecture about why we should stay put. At one point I cast a sidelong glance at Pam and saw a single, hot tear trickle down her cheek. Poor, tender-hearted, one-man Pam, all she heard of my lecture was, "Pam, sometimes I think you've got the wrong guy, blah blah blah blah blah blah blah, and furthermore blah blah blah blah blah."

Ah well, no doubt by now you have a sense of the sort of character you're dealing with, and feel no surprise at my boorish and insensitive behaviour. The thing is, a part of me still sympathizes with those sentiments. I agree with myself. Somehow in North America we've gone horribly wrong and have become a nation of consumers rather than producers, silly creatures with no direction or purpose in life except accumulation and recreation. My idea has always been to put the emphasis on production rather than consumption, to define myself by what I produce, not what I consume (to write racy, sharp-end books rather than buying a sports car, say, or a motorcycle). I'm not saying I have all the answers, and I agree I could have expressed myself more diplomatically to Pam, who, after all, was just looking for a cozy nook for her as-yet-to-be-conceived child. But that's the way I've always lived my life, for better or worse. Be yourself, do what comes naturally, blurt out what's on your mind, then the next day phone (or in extreme cases, write) and apologize.

At the time, we were living in a loft above a bar called The Devil's Martini, which turned out to be aptly named: a junior-management watering (hell-)hole and meat market where drunken former frat boys, fresh out of college, shot pool and tried to pick up their sexy secretaries. In fact, when I stop to think about it, I realize that all the places I've lived in have been fiendishly appropriate. During my Bachelor Hell phase, when a woman might wander in through my open front door in the middle of the night and crawl into bed with me, I lived above a store called The Get It On Boutique. After that, during the heaviest drinking phase of my life (I was celebrating meeting Pam), I lived above a bar called The Devil's Martini. Now I live across the street from a mental-health facility. . . .

I've always liked loft living. I'm a big fellow, as I may have mentioned, heavy-footed, clumsy. I've always liked large, rough-hewn spaces with not too much dainty furniture to stumble into and perhaps destroy—and no walls. "Why does the bourgeoisie feel it needs walls?" I would often ask—rhetorically, I feel.

But it turns out there are actually a number of good reasons why walls have been developed over the centuries. Privacy, for one. The walls of the bathroom didn't reach the ceiling, so when we had guests we had to go down to The Devil's Martini to take a dump (we went down so much, we called it "the rec room"). And I found that if Pam was on the phone, I couldn't write or nap, my two favourite activities. We had numerous arguments around that, so many that Pam now refers to this period as a bad patch in our relationship.

It's funny how real estate and relationships are linked, don't you think? Now that we have a house with walls, and doors you can shut, not to mention separate phone lines, we don't have those arguments anymore. We have *other* arguments, as you will see, but we don't have those anymore (these days, we mostly argue over the thermostat: she wants to turn it up, I want to turn it down). If Pam's talking on the phone, I can go to another part of the house and shut the door. And that's been another important discovery: you can't necessarily reinvent everything in your lifetime. It took generations to invent things like walls, cooking, the fork, each scrap of knowledge passed down from mother or father to son or daughter, and sometimes you simply have to defer to that.

After looking at probably a hundred dumps, we finally found this house, the house I presently husband, a crumbling, three-storey Victorian across from the Queen Street Mental Health Centre. A starkly uninhabitable pile of bricks, to most people's way of thinking. In fact, some of our friends exulted behind our backs over what a horrible mistake we'd made. "You should see the dump Pam and

Dave bought!" a couple of people said (it got back to me through the grapevine). The former owner had been a pensioner whose wife was completely crazy. She would perch on what the real estate agent called the "Juliet balcony" at the front of the house and scream obscenities at the children walking to and from school. And he was no Prince Charming either, the neighbours intimated. He beat her, they hinted; sometimes they could even hear the thumps and thuds through the walls.

"An old wife-beater's house," I kept saying to myself, over and over. "We bought an old wife-beater's house."

When the wife died, he let the house crumble and rot around him. It wasn't that the linoleum on the floor was worn in spots; there were only islands of linoleum that weren't worn. We thought the windows to a door in the living room had been painted brown for privacy, but when we scratched and sniffed it, it turned out to be nicotine—and he'd quit smoking in 1963.

But the floor in between the linoleum islands was nice hardwood, the ceilings were high, and we were young, were we not? Young and full of energy. With a little elbow grease and some rented steamers and sanders, we could whip the place into shape lickety-split. "I could renovate the whole house in six weeks with a crowbar and a case of tequila," I frequently boasted to bemused smiles and sardonic snickering. (I'm not really all that handy. . . .)

With my typical luck, five days after we signed the papers for the house, I got a call from the Über-boss at my local TV news station regarding my two-day-a-week job. "It's not good news, I'm afraid," she said. "Budget cuts . . . can't use you . . . be happy to recommend . . ." Nothing personal, according to her (although I suppose she could have found me a spot if she had really wanted me). They were making cuts in the Cosmodemonic staff, and I was probably one of the last part-timers in the place. Part-timers always walk the plank first. It's crazy, I think, because they're cheap. You don't even have to pay them benefits. But of course, you don't own a part-timer's soul, so sooner or later they have to go, right? Personally, I dream of a glorious, golden future where everyone is a part-timer, and we spend all our free time cultivating our families and our individuality (and we all live downtown in low-rise six-plexes)—but my dream is a long way off, I realize.

Before the phone call, I had been thinking what a mug's game freelance writing is. A treadmill to nowhere: you work hard, rise to the top of your profession, perhaps, and where does it get you? Nowhere. The chance to do more of the same, ad infinitum.

"Don't worry about it, Dave," Pam said, one glorious, golden day. "You write your book. I'll pay the bills for a while."

4. "I AM A HOUSEHUSBAND"

I remember the first time I uttered those words in public, in response to the omnipresent, pestilential question, "What do you do?" I said it out of malice—malice and the desire to draw attention to myself, as you will see. But saying those words had a curiously liberating effect.

I was at a wedding—best wedding I've been to, I often tell people, and it's true. We skinny-dipped at the reception. How often can you say that? Isn't that a beautiful sentence? My friend Felicia was marrying a jazz musician/Web site designer in a little wooden church near her family's ultra-rustic, handed-down-through-the-generations family cabin, with reception to follow at a nearby island. A burning, searing day: the sun crackled and popped in the sky above, we sweated and steamed in our monkey suits and party dresses on the earth below. "Bring your bathing suits and swim at the reception," the invitation had said, but in the pre-wedding kerfuffle, of course, everyone forgot. We were debating what to do when the bride herself bustled by in full quasi-medieval regalia.

"Don't worry about it," she said. "Skinny-dip."

What more sanction do you need? We walked down to a dock around the corner and away from the main reception area, doffed our duds and dived in the drink. Men and women alike. A real sixties scene, except the men all had short hair and the women, naked and treading water, discussed problems at the office.

Very refreshing. The reception was quite refreshing, too; in fact I may have been a tad too well refreshed, because memories of the latter half of that reception come back only in strobe-lit flashes. But I already had a girlfriend, so I didn't have to try to pick anyone up, and I didn't have to make a speech, so why not fill my boots? I'd been too poor for too long to start turning down free booze, especially fine wines. When the great aviator Joseph LeBrix (first non-stop crossing of the Atlantic, in 1927) was rescued from a crash in the desert, he swore that in his delirium he had seen parade before his eyes every glass of frosted beer he had refused in his life; and that's the way I feel about free booze, I guess. People talk a lot about starving writers. But no one ever mentions the terrible thirst that can come over a youngish man of literary pretensions who can't even afford a bottle of plonk, let alone the incomparable joy of an ice-cold Gibson mixed by a talented bartender in swish surroundings.

I remember speeches; posing in front of a trompe l'oeil

backdrop for pictures; bumping over the treacherous waters of Go Home Lake in a speedboat with some other guests after the reception, a certain Rick at the helm, navigating by the light of a fading flashlight; a last late-night skinny dip with my friend and editor Doug P., thinking how thin and fit he looked as he dove in, then throwing my own fat, pale body off the dock, while the girls (Pam and Doug's future wife Sue) stood naked and shivering on the dock, hugging themselves and stamping their feet, trying to work up the courage to enter the inky water; then all is darkness.

The next morning there was a brunch en plein air on the patio outside the cottage. The brunch was presided over by none other than the paterfamilias himself, the patriarch, the grand old man, the lord of the manor, the head of the household—Felicia's father, in other words.

He'd been drunker than I was the night before (at least, I *hope* he was) and *he*'d given a speech. It was . . . not distinguished. In fact, may I pause for a moment here to give three pieces of advice if you have to give a speech at a wedding? 1) Don't get drunk first; 2) Never try to "wing it"; 3) Never, ever do both. Both Felicia's father and brother contravened all three tenets of wedding speech–making, and the results, in my opinion, were disastrous.

First up was Felicia's brother. Mumbling and muttering only semi-intelligibly, he paced up and down the platform with the microphone in his hand, speaking of youthful indiscretions, ancient rivalries, alluding darkly to family skeletons. "Phew, that was weird," we all thought when he finally ended, or abandoned, his speech.

Then her father assumed the stage.

"Felicia was never the most intelligent or attractive of my offspring," his speech began and actually managed to go downhill from there. Rambling, dilatory, mostly about himself—"Talk about the bride!" someone heckled at one point—it was the single worst wedding speech I've witnessed, and I've seen some face-grabbers. As this old dog brayed into the night, two things became abundantly clear: 1) like so many self-appointed great men, he knew his own offspring hardly at all; 2) he was jealous of his daughter's career. A lifelong high-level government bureaucrat, now retired, he'd always nursed the ambition to write, but never got around to it. Why not? Same old story: he didn't want to give up his fat paycheque and the cushy lifestyle it afforded him. A speech fraught with Oedipal overtones— or not Oedipal, since that refers to mother-son relations. Perhaps it's better to say: an Electra-fying speech.

For most of the brunch he ignored us, Felicia's friends, whom he called "the children" despite the fact we were all in our late twenties and early thirties, and addressed his own age group, his cohort, delivering various veiled barbs and oblique observations that seemed designed to convey the message: "Although I never wrote my great book, it is as much the world's loss as mine." All in all, he struck me as one of those who thinks this is his movie, a movie about a swashbuckling former bureaucrat and man about town who, though he never picked up the pen, is still known as a raconteur and wit; the rest of us are merely extras, background blobs you can barely make out as the camera pans past.

Such, in any case, were my conclusions as I sat, stewing and fuming, a bundle of malice, at my end of the table, trying to think what I could blurt out that would persuade him that this was actually *my* movie, a movie about a youngish boulevardier and man about town who, although he had yet to complete his great works, was nonetheless obviously destined for a glittering career; and *he*, the Great Raconteur, was the extra, or at best a cameo or walk-on.

My chance came halfway through the meal. The Great Raconteur was bragging and boasting to his audience that he'd "never felt comfortable" with the perquisites of government work, such as the fact he could travel anywhere by train for free (he didn't say that he never travelled by train, or that he always paid for his tickets, he just "never felt comfortable" about it).

"I don't agree with you there," I piped up from the other end of the table. "I've been working for a government-funded television station for the past five years, and I think government fat tastes delicious, *just like chicken*."

"Jes' . . . lahk . . . chickin," I repeated in a southern-fried accent, shamelessly stealing a line from my own as-yet-unpublished novel.

My statement didn't have the desired effect, of convincing him it was my movie, but it did manage to derail the conversation into a brief debate on the merits versus the demerits of government-funded television before the Great Raconteur steered it back to its main topic—himself. I think my red-herring comment stuck in his craw somehow, though, for he gazed around at "the children," clapped his hands together and said, "So. Who are you all? What do you do?"

With an expectant eyebrow-arch, he turned to the person immediately to his left. Oh no, I realized with mounting panic, he's going to go around the table and ask each of us what we do for a living. He expects each of us to bark out our professions like trained Pekingese or circus seals. Roof, roof! I'm a roofer, sir! Arr, arr! I'm an architect!

What am I going to say? I wondered. I couldn't say I was a writer, not in this crowd, which included several luminaries of Canadian publishing and even Felicia's bigshot agent from New York. I couldn't handle the inevitable follow-up: "Oh, really? Who do you write for?" I had to think of something fast. Next to me, to my right, Pam was saying, "I'm a television r-r-r-reporter, sir."

Then it was my turn. All eyes turned my way. A deathly silence fell over the crowd, as usual, and, as usual, the veins, arteries and capillaries of my head immediately became engorged with hot blood.

But in a flash, it came to me what I had to do. Rather than fill the air with empty brags and boasts, I would go the other way (the only way that was in fact open to me): humility.

"I am a househusband," I said simply.

"I thought you said you worked in television?"

"Oh, yes, well, I did, but I was fired. Or laid off, or whatever. They *said* it wasn't anything personal. Anyway," I said, face on fire now, looping my arm around Pam like a drowning man clutching a life preserver, "Pam's the breadwinner. I cook and do . . . things around the house."

A typical David Eddie performance: a bad idea, poorly executed. However, my blurtaceous remarks seemed to melt the curmudgeonly crust of the Great Raconteur.

"Well, that's what I am too, I suppose," he said, after a thoughtful pause, "now that I'm retired: a househusband." And then he turned his attention to the next person, thank God.

We were both lying, of course—or perhaps it's kinder to say we were kidding ourselves and everyone else. Sitting around the house all day, getting underfoot and moaning and complaining while your wife continues to do all the cleaning, cooking and everything else (as I imagined to be the case for the Great Raconteur) hardly qualify you as a househusband. Of course, neither does hanging around the apartment while your girlfriend goes to work, typing at a typewriter, taking naps, making yourself sandwiches and meeting your friends for coffee (my lifestyle). It makes you a leech, a mooch, a son-in-law from hell, a *jazz musician* of the type Marilyn Monroe is trying to avoid in the movie *Some Like It Hot*, so she can snag a millionaire.

In my defence though: a) I wrote a book; b) my household skills were slowly evolving. After two years of living together, I was still a little hazy on which was recycling and which garbage night, and I still believed in the Toilet Paper Fairy (she replaces the rolls while you sleep); but at least I was able to provide a hot meal for Pam when she came home from work.

Then, as per the terms of our agreement, Pam and I pulled the goalie (as we say in Canada) and started having sex without birth control. Actually, Pam had been off the pill for some time. She kept referring to a diaphragm that never seemed to materialize. Her diaphragm was "in the mail," and in the meantime we practised the savage art of withdrawal. Like a porn star I would pull out in jittery haste at the last second, spraying doomed sperm everywhere, leaving Pam twisting in the wind, orgasm-wise, clawing the empty air, angry and frustrated, as I subsided, sated, next to her. Now though, as decreed, this samurai-like practice would come to an end.

One morning—January 17, 1996, to be precise—I awoke late, with the cat biting my nose, pretending to lick but slipping in little nips, so I'd wake up and feed her. I put on my specs and stared at the clock: 10:30 A.M.

"Damn, Pam," I said to the snoozing lump next to me. "I'll never get a W. Somerset Maugham routine going at this rate."

W. Somerset Maugham had an ironclad routine. He was at his desk at exactly 9:30 every morning and wrote until 12:55, at which point he had exactly one martini. After dinner, he might have a single brandy, then refuse a second "in such a way as you knew not to offer it again." Likewise, after dinner, he smoked two cigarettes, hungrily, quickly, then always refused a third "in such a way as you knew not to offer it again."

Thanks in part to his disciplined lifestyle, Maugham enjoyed a productive and successful sixty-year career, at the end of which he lived in a mansion in Cap-Ferrat, on the Côte d'Azur, with a pool and thirteen servants (not including his lover/amanuensis Gerald): a cook, two maids, a butler, a footman, a chauffeur, and seven gardeners.

Seven gardeners! I jumped out of bed and headed downstairs, clapping my hands together, my internal monologue stuck on a self-flagellation tape-loop: Get your *shit* together; you're screwing *up*; you've got to bust your *hump* if you want to get to the *top*. I fed the cat, grabbed the paper and checked out the mail. My unemployment cheque arrived (phew). I headed back upstairs, to the bathroom. Just then, Pam was coming downstairs with her pregnancy test kit in her hand, and we met at the door.

"Can I go first?" she said. "You have to use your first urine of the day, and I really have to go."

I really had to go, too, but she had me trumped. Prospective pregnancy automatically gives you the moral high ground, so I said OK and headed downstairs where, I confess, I pissed in the sink. Some old bachelor habits die hard.

I tried to make some coffee. My mother had given us a home espresso machine, and it worked really well—at first. For the first few months we had delicious cappuccinos every morning. But now it seemed . . . tired. Maybe I wasn't cleaning it properly, or maybe the pump was becoming worn out, or both; but it made coffee more and more slowly each day. On this particular morning— a morning on which I would have loved a delicious cappuccino, it was working worse than ever. It took nearly ten minutes to coax a muddy half inch out of the constipated contraption.

"Argh!" I expostulated in exasperation when Pam came into the kitchen.

"What is it?" she asked me.

"This espresso machine is driving me crazy! It's only releasing one drop of coffee every fifteen seconds. It's like Chinese water torture! I don't understand it. I clean it all the time, but it just gets worse! I know my mother gave it to us and everything, but I think we're going to have to throw it out—it'll cost too much to fix—and go back to filtered coffee. You know, you're supposed to drink filtered coffee anyway. You're only supposed to have espresso-style coffee once in a while, as a special treat."

"Really?" Pam said. "Why?"

"Filtered coffee's less carcinogenic. The filter takes out the most carcinogenic oils; whereas with espresso-style coffee—cappuccinos, lattes, etc.—you get them all."

"Hmph, I didn't know that," Pam said. Then, "Aren't you curious about the results of my pregnancy test?"

"Oh, yes, sorry. How'd it go?"

"Well, I'm pregnant."

"Oh. Congratulations!" I said and gave her a big hug. It might seem like an odd thing to say, but I was really happy for her. And for myself, too, of course.

Pam's a healthy girl. The main symptoms of her pregnancy were she was a) ravenous and b) emotional. These two factors came together in an incident, my favourite story from Pam's pregnancy, that took place on the road to Max's cottage. I'd been feeding her all sorts of healthy foods: risotto, soups, roast chicken, vegetables, fruit and nuts. But on the way up to Max's cottage she got a real craving for her favourite junk food: a grease bomb on two discs of white death with a side order of fat-saturated coffin nails, all washed down with artificially flavoured, carbonated sugar-water (burger, fries and soft drink, in other words).

All the way up she was talking about it, how much she was looking forward to it, how she would like it prepared, the relative merits and demerits of the burgers of various fast-food chains and why this particular type of double-decker burger (slathered in what in my opinion is a revolting tartar-like sauce) is pre-eminent among them all. As the family chef, I was feeling a tad insulted. Why did she never talk about my dinners in this way? Often when I served my creations she would say, "Mmmm . . . delicious," but further elaboration was rare.

Finally we made it to the drive-through, and after carefully considering pictures of our possible options displayed on a signpost, enunciated our orders into the intercom, pulled up to the window and grabbed our bag, already attractively mottled with grease.

Our usual routine in these situations was I would take all the components of our fast-food meal and arrange them on the dashboard or gearshift console so she could drive. (I don't drive; I'm too absent-minded. The few years I did have a licence, I was always thinking about something else and crashing into things—all inanimate, luckily. But I knew it was only a matter of time before the day came when I'd be checking my hair in the rear-view just as some old lady stepped in front of my speeding grille; so I let my licence lapse as a public service.) Unfortunately, just as we were accelerating onto the highway, I bobbled the burger. For a horrible moment, I was juggling all the ingredients—patties, buns, lettuce, tomato— in mid air. Then they all landed on the floor in a quickly coagulating heap.

"I *knew* you were going to do that. I knew it," Pam said and burst into tears accompanied by such heart-rending sobs that we had to pull over, as I frantically tried to reassemble her burger.

"I'm sorry, Pam. I really am," I said over and over, as our car sat angled on the shoulder.

"It's all right, Dave," she said through her sobs. "I just . . . wanted it so badly."

I put her burger together and handed it to her.

After a pause, she said, munching bravely, still sniffling a bit, "It's actually not that bad."

So we wouldn't have to live in a refrigerator box during Pam's maternity leave, I hustled up a job—as a radio producer this time.

I heard, or rather overheard, about it at yet another book launch party. I hate those things, but you have to show your face from time to time, right? This one was for a book I didn't particularly care about, all about two peat-pitchers on the Isle of Skye. The story was told in some sort of quasi-Gaelic dialect, and I couldn't make head or tail of it. But of course critics hailed it "Best Book Ever Written," juries showered prizes on the author's humble head, rights had been sold everywhere from Burkina Faso to Bangladesh; and it was being made into a movie.

I was leaning against the bar, thinking of a quote from the apophthegmata of the Desert Fathers, "Woe to the man whose fame is bigger than his works"; and other bitter, envious thoughts, when I overheard a balding, timid-looking fellow telling a Random House publicist that he'd inherited some money and was quitting his job as books producer at a radio station, and they didn't know how they were going to replace him.

Normally at this point, I would simply have grabbed my beer and staggered off slack-jawed to join a couple of my cronies. But since Pam was pregnant, I collared this timid-looking fellow like a vice cop, practically slammed him against the wall as I fired one question after another at him: What do you mean they don't know who's going to replace you? Can anyone apply? Who's your boss? How can I get in touch with him or her? And, incidentally, how much did you inherit? He wouldn't answer that last one, but he was very gracious, helpful and forthcoming on all other matters.

To make a long story short, I didn't get his job, but I did get another one. The secret to the success of my quixotic campaign against the ramparts of radio was bribery, I think—bribery, loquacity and lying about my age. At the first interview, the big boss, the Executive Producer of All Radio News and Current Affairs, went on and on about how they needed more people under thirty-five. She wanted to assemble a whole team of people under thirty-five. They needed to be hipper, more in touch with what's going on and so on. Then she asked me how old I was.

". . . thirty-four," I said, like an idiot, shaving a single, stupid year off my age. But what could I do? It seemed extremely important to this woman, and I really wanted the job. My wife was pregnant, people! Afterwards, I sent not just a thank-you note, but also a thank-you bottle of wine (*appellation Bordeaux supérieure contrôlée*) to the Executive Producer of All Radio News and Current Affairs.

"Shameless!" Max spluttered when I told him about my bribe. "Outrageous! Over-the-top!" But can you ever be too shameless and over-the-top when it comes to humanity's infinite tolerance for bootlicking, butt-kissing and kowtowing? I made it to the next level of interviews, what more do I need to say? I was "boarded" by a team of three people, which they only do when they're very interested.

"Tell us a bit about yourself," they asked me after we'd all settled down.

"Well, I'm a bit of an oddball," I began and launched into an hour-long monologue about my hair-raising adventures in other jobs, throwing in a couple of non-job situations for spice. They chuckled gratifyingly the whole time. They liked me, I think, and, more than that, it was a relief for them not to have to do any work: here was an interviewee who was pretty much interviewing himself. I entertained them, or as my friend Jill said, "Some people lowball in interviews. Some people highball. You *oddballed* them."

True enough. And although I didn't send any of them a bottle of wine, they wound up hiring me. Not for the book-booking job, but for another, similar position on another show—and strictly temporary, as usual. I was a "summer student," on a two-month contract, with option to renew.

At age thirty-five, I was a "summer student." I loved that job, though. The politics were brutal, as usual. My colleagues were all extremely bright and talented, but they'd obviously been working together too long. The weekly meetings were pure torture, pure Artaudian theatre of cruelty. The Executive Producer would go around the table, asking each producer for his/her story ideas. Blushing, glancing at notes or at a newspaper or magazine article, the producer would tentatively propose a possible story idea, whereupon everyone else would immediately shoot it down with poisoned arrows, barbed comments and ad hominem attacks. The target of the attack would then stew and fume and nurse his/her wounds, until it was his/her turn to exact revenge. This process had obviously been going on for *years*. One guy, who'd been there twenty-five years, and who complained constantly about his health and walked around in tiny shorts, showing off his bandy, gouty legs, simply read the newspaper throughout the whole meeting. Every once in a while from behind the rustling pages, he would say in his high, piping voice, "I'm getting that why-should-I-care? feeling again." (A real prince. He wrote a book of poetry back in the 1960s, and when he found out I had a book coming out, said to me, "Wait till you see your book on the remainder table. Then you'll know what it means to be an author!" And later, after Nicholas was born: "The best way to quiet a crying baby down is with a ball-peen hammer between the eyes.")

The whole work environment in general struck me as sick at its very core. In *A Moveable Feast*, Ernest Hemingway exhorts himself to "write one true sentence. Write the truest sentence that you know," and I guess mine would be: *We live wrong.* Take lunch, for example. Lunch should be something you eat on a marble table under a grape arbour somewhere in the hills of Abruzzi, with bowls of olives and bottles of unlabelled wine on the table. But what is lunch for modern man, *Homo buttcoveris in cubiculo*? An elevator ride followed by an escalator ride to the Food Court in the basement of a skyscraper, where *Homo buttcoveris* is confronted with a choice between quickie Italian, quickie Thai, quickie Chinese, quickie Indian and quickie American—fast food, in short, to be scarfed down alone, while sitting at a plastic table, staring into space.

But the actual work itself I enjoyed very much. It was one of those rare jobs where you actually learn things and improve your mind. I had to come up with story ideas for radio segments about anything from the news, culture, *Zeitgeist*, world of ideas or academia—"whatever interests *you*, Dave," as the executive producer of the show, my boss's boss and therefore my boss (she didn't hire me, but she had the power to fire me) would say. It was one of those jobs where I could be sitting at my desk, my feet propped up, reading a novel, and if my boss passed by she would only say mildly, "How's the book coming, Dave?"

And I was doing well at it, apparently. Towards the end of my two-month contract, my boss asked me into her office. "That's it. I'm finished," I thought, already gathering up my things in my mind. But she surprised me by renewing my contract for two more months, heaping praise on my head for what she kept calling my "learning curve."

"And we need more young people around here, Dave," she said, just like the exec had at our initial interview. "I keep telling people, unless we get more young people in here, we're going to lose touch with what's going on."

"You know, I'm not all that young," I said on this occasion, for some unknown reason. "I'm thirty-five," I said, telling the truth this time.

"Well, that's a sad comment on this place that that seems young," she said. "Do you realize the average age around here is forty-eight and rising?"

I was surprised it was that low. Because of their policy of last-hired, first-fired, the place was like a Jurassic nursing home. Every once in a while they'd hire a token young person, but only temporarily, and with a few exceptions they usually got the heave-ho within a few months. The ones who were left *were* totally out of touch. They drove back and forth to their jobs from the suburbs and knew nothing about the world except what their newspapers and televisions told them.

But I kept these observations to myself, simply raised my eyebrows and tried to look surprised.

"Anyway, you're from a different culture," she said, referring, no doubt, to my goatee and vintage/homeboy wardrobe.

I liked my job, for once they seemed to like me and, I have to admit, I liked making money. Why not? I'm only human. I liked being able to pick up the tab for drinks without a second thought. I liked being able to buy myself a shirt without going into a tailspin of self-loathing and self-recrimination; I liked feeling like an earner, a breadwinner for my huge-and-growing-huger-every-day wife. It felt good to be the rock on which Pam could depend.

Especially when it was all so *easy*. Jobs are a *scam*, I thought, as I always do when I have one. All anyone around me seemed to be doing was socializing, chatting on the phone, e-mailing each other and playing Solitaire or Doom on their computers. They worked maybe two hours a day. The rest was all hot air, but, of course they hung around eternally, pretending to work. And for this, a quite sizable chunk of cash was direct-deposited into their accounts every two weeks. "Freelancing is for *suckers*," I said to myself, cursing myself for being an idiot because I hadn't realized this sooner.

But as the weeks rolled by, and the blob of protoplasm that was later to become Nicholas grew inside Pam's belly, Pam and I held a number of discussions and in the end agreed on a series of near-Pythagorean truths: 1) Pam made more money than I did; 2) she had ten years invested in her career, whereas I only had a few months; 3) I wanted to be a writer, anyway; 4) we didn't want to put him in daycare.

"I love him already," Pam would say, patting her pregnant belly. "It just doesn't feel right to hand him over to strangers after only a couple of months."

"I'll take care of him," I said—and with that simple statement made the decision to become a *true* househusband and stay-at-home dad.

5. THE ADVENT
OF NICHOLAS

It is true, is it not, that in this life months and years go by where nothing at all happens, and then bam, bam, bam—everything happens all at once. Around the time of Nicholas's scheduled arrival into the world there was a welter of events: my father's prostate operation; getting fired; and the launch of my novel, *Chump Change*.

By nerve-wracking coincidence, Nicholas's due date—September 19, 1996—was the same day scheduled for the launch of *Chump Change*. As the day approached, I had all the usual worries, I suppose, a first-time author has around a launch party. Would enough media show up? Do I have enough friends that whatever media *does* show up will perceive me as a happening guy? Should I invite any big shots and, if so, which ones (too many big shots can kill a party, because they all act so bored)? Added to these concerns was the mental picture of Pam clutching her stomach just as the ceremonies were getting under way, me leaning into the mike and saying, over the screech of a feedback loop, "Ladies and gentlemen, I'm sorry, I have to leave. My wife's in the final stages of labour, and we have to rush to the hospital. But thanks for the support. Have plenty of snacks and drinks, and enjoy yourselves."

As it happened, though, Nicholas hung on in the cozy comfort of Pam's womb an extra week, and I didn't have to make any sudden announcements. Plenty of people showed up, and *Chump Change* was launched into the world in a gratifying glare of media, although Pam threatened to steal the whole show with her late-pregnancy radiance. She was 8.9999 months pregnant and *beaming*, gentlemen. She looked like she had TV lights trained on her even when she didn't. It was almost embarrassing. In her floral maternity dress, she was a still centre of peace, calm and rootedness in the midst of a raging storm of frantic schmoozing.

A couple of weeks before, I'd visited my father in the hospital, where he was recovering from an operation for prostate cancer. Not such a big deal, in his case. "Catch cancer early," American kids were told (somewhat ambiguously, if you ask me) when my father was growing up, and he took this advice to heart. He was particularly worried about prostate cancer, so after he turned fifty-five or so, he started getting himself checked regularly, sometimes even over the pooh-poohing of his general practitioner. So sure enough, when they detected cancer, it was just a tiny node, not too aggressive—or *ambitious*, as I heard someone else's tumour described recently.

A minor operation—but also an intrusive one, because they go in from the front and have to push aside all sorts of internal organs and wiring (all slick with blood and marbled with fat, in my mental picture) to get at the prostate. So I think Dad was a tad miffed that I hadn't visited before the operation, only after, when he was recuperating. I can't explain this lapse in filial loyalty and punctilio. I guess I was too wrapped up in my own problems.

He was quite gracious about it, though. When I came to visit, he was sucking on ice chips. For the moisture, he explained, though I didn't understand then, and still don't now, why ice chips are better than unfrozen water. He had a bowl of ice chips on his stomach, and from time to time he would pop one into his mouth and suck on it or crunch it between his teeth.

His girlfriend, or, if you prefer, common-law wife, was there, too (my mother and father are divorced). The three of us talked a bit about the impending birth of Nicholas, how Pam was feeling, and then the conversation got around to how I was feeling about it all.

"Tell him, Scotty," Dad's girlfriend said, nudging him. "Tell him how you felt when *he* was born. How you felt when you had your first-born son."

Dad hesitated a second. These kinds of avowals aren't really his style. But after sucking thoughtfully on his ice chip for a couple of moments, he said in his lugubrious drawl, "Well, Dave, it's a feeling of love that starts in your toes and goes right through you."

I was touched by his sentiment, and as a dutiful son I thought over his words carefully and committed them to memory. But it didn't turn out that way for me. Maybe I'm just a cold-hearted bastard. Or maybe it's simply that times have changed. After all, my father's first glimpse of me was probably through the glass window of the maternity ward, after I had been cleaned up, whereas I was present at the actual moment of Nicholas's birth. And, I have to admit, my first glimpse of Nicholas inspired me mostly with horror.

I was down at the end of the bed, snapping pictures. Originally, I had been holding Pam's hand, but at the last minute, someone (I think it was my mother) shoved me aside and said, "Here he comes! Take a picture!" I did as I was told. Then the midwife said, "Here he is!" I peered into the "vaginal opening." The bit of his head that I could see was dark grey and ridged, like some sort of sci-fi alien (babies' heads become compressed, forming ridges on top, so they can squeeze through the birth canal, and they're covered in vernix, a slimy grey goo that acts as a lubricant).

"Oh, my God," I remember thinking. "He looks like a dead thing. Pam's giving birth to a dead thing." I knew, of course, from all the electrical equipment in the room that he was alive, but this refrain kept going through my brain. His head popped out from between Pam's legs, and he glared angrily around the room, resembling nothing so much, it seemed to me, as an old man looking for a waitress he thinks is avoiding him. Then the rest of him came sliding out in a slippery, slithering rush. And of course, after that the afterbirth came flying out—the placenta, about which the less said the better, I think, and from which, gentlemen, I suggest, if you're present at the birth, you avert your eyes.

The next thing I felt towards Nicholas was respect. Here he'd gone through one of the most dramatic and wrenching changes life has to offer—second only, perhaps, to death—and he didn't even cry. Just a short "Waah!" and then he fell silent as he looked blinkingly around the room with his brand-new eyes, taking it all in. He cried a bit when they gave him a vitamin K shot, but still not much.

"Cool customer," I thought. "I like that."

Also I thought him extremely beautiful. He had, and has, heart-shaped nostrils and long, expressive fingers. I was amazed my booze-soaked, drug-addled sperm could produce such an outstanding specimen of *Homo sapiens*. Pam probably has some special sort of scrubbers that eliminate all impurities and imperfections as the sperm swim along, I said to myself. Sort of like a car wash, I decided.

He'll need an agent, was my next thought. One of my exes has a friend whose kid was in diaper commercials and raked in forty thousand dollars in his first year of life. More than I've made in any year of *my* life.

And then I felt anxiety and protectiveness towards him and hoped he would always be warm and dry in this world and find happiness.

But love? I don't remember feeling any of that. Pam loved him before she even laid eyes on him. She loved him in utero, and as soon as he was born they started looking at each other with goo-goo eyes and haven't stopped. But Nicholas and I were strangers. Learning to love one another would take time.

But time, as it turned out, was something I was destined to have. Shortly after Nicholas was born, my schedule freed up quite a bit.

Nicholas was born on a Thursday night, so naturally I took Friday off. But I was expected to show up for work on

Monday. In that mostly female, childless office, they had no concept of paternity leave. In fact, it hardly seemed to register on my colleagues that I had a kid at all. A major, life-changing event for me; a dimly perceived detail for them. A couple of people mumbled their congratulations, but, for the most part it was business as usual. People kept their heads down and pretended to be busy, e-mailed friends and murmured into the phone on urgent personal calls.

On Tuesday, I got whacked. That's just the word for it. I don't know if you've seen the movie *GoodFellas*, but there's a scene in it where Joe Pesci thinks he's going to "get made"—become a boss—but instead he's led into a tiled room with a drain in the floor, and a table with empty chairs around it. Turns out he pissed off one too many people and killed a made man over a minor dispute. Hubris. "Oh, no," he says, just as phut, he gets it in the back of the head from a gun with a silencer.

That's how it happened with me. The Executive Producer of All Radio News and Current Affairs called me and my immediate boss, a woman who wore an L.L. Bean barn jacket to work every day, into her office for what I thought was a routine meeting and started feeling me out with a few questions. After a while, though, the questions became more adversarial in tone. What was I working on? Why didn't I have more stories on "the board" (a large board with the names of the various stories and the producers working on them written in felt pen). What was happening?

My eyes slid over to Mrs. L.L. Bean Jacket, thinking, "You can jump in any time here." She was, after all, the bottleneck. She was giving me the runaround on all my stories, and every time I went into her office to talk about them she quickly switched the topic to her personal life, launching into long, boring stories about her family, her teenage son, even the fucking family dog. We were "friends," supposedly; I even walked her to her car once. She'd just been promoted from producer to boss of the producers, and I think she was out of her depth; that, or she felt uncomfortable in the role of boss.

To my horror, though, her face wore the same look of curious expectancy as the Executive Producer. Oh, no, I thought, like Joe Pesci, and felt the (metaphorical) cold muzzle of the silencer against the back of my cranium. I started explaining about this story, that story, but I knew I was finished. While I was talking, Mrs. L.L. Bean Jacket stood up as if suddenly remembering something and left the room.

I was left alone with the Exec. That's when she said, "Dave, I'm afraid I can't renew your contract any further."

For some reason, though, like an executive producer in a nightmare, she continued to ask me questions about my story ideas. She was like a dog on a bone, gnawing, worrying, especially about a story I'd proposed about a book called *Hermits*. A beautiful book, in my opinion, simple, profound, often quite funny, about the history of eremitism, or living in seclusion from social life, at least for a while. And the author, Peter France, was a hermit himself, although not the popular notion of a wild-eyed, hirsute madman. He had been a BBC (TV) producer, who at one point was famous enough to be recognized when he walked down the street. But he had chucked the job and now lived with his wife on the island of Patmos, in the middle of the Aegean Sea. In the morning, he wrote and she painted.

It sounded like a great life to me. One of my last acts as a radio producer was to interview him over the phone, through special arrangement with his publisher. He and his wife had just come in from a swim in the Aegean, and were having a glass of wine. I'm always fascinated by how people make it without working, so I asked him that. He said he'd saved a little money from his BBC days, and they kept their overhead low.

I pitched this idea hard at what turned out to be my last-ever story meeting; but, as usual, it was shot down in a hail of abuse.

Now the Executive Producer was saying, "That hermit story idea, for example. Tell me why I should care about that."

Wearily, I tried to explain. A lot of people were looking for greater simplicity in their lives, I said. They were tired of excess, wanted to lower their overheads and refocus their lives. And the urge to be alone has always been with us, warring against our natural need for society. When Aristotle said, "Man is by nature a political animal," he didn't mean that we're born to take part in party politics, but that it is our nature to live in a polis, or community. But there's always been the counter-urge to get away from people, put one's spiritual house in order, acquire wisdom and seek God. I mentioned Lao-tzu, Thomas Merton, the poet Robert Lax, a contemporary of Ginsberg's who also lives on Patmos, and the earliest Christian monks, the Desert Fathers.

"These people believed solitude is no less than the mother of wisdom," I concluded. "And many returned to society to share their insights. Jesus, for example, retired to the desert but returned to share what he learned there."

"But how does any of that relate to ordinary working people?" she asked. "For example, how would that relate to someone like *me*, who gets up and comes to work every day? Can you explain why someone like *me* should care about hermits?"

I looked at her in her freeze-dried hair-helmet, pink suit and horse-and-buggy brooch.

"No," I said. "I can't."

I snapped my notes shut, stood up and walked out of her office. The meeting was over and so was my radio career.

The moral of this story, boys and girls, is: beware of nice, chatty yuppies in L.L. Bean jackets. They might act like your friends, tell you all sorts of long-winded anecdotes about their families, but the minute there's even a whiff of threat to their own security, they'll knife you. Their consciences don't trouble them, because their only loyalty is to those same families. "I did it for the sake of my family" is a phrase that has been used, I believe, to justify more evil in the history of humanity than even "I did it for my country" or "I did it for my religion."

Who needed their mouldy old radio job, anyway? (Later, Mrs. L.L. Bean Jacket would sidle up to me and ask where I got that hermit idea, because they were thinking of using it for the show.) I was a published author now—and, besides, hadn't I already made the decision to stay home with Nick?

Pam stayed home with him full-time for two months, and with the money I'd saved from my job, plus my unemployment cheques, we figured we could keep afloat for six months.

She didn't want to take any more time off than that, ladies. Television news is a shark-eat-shark business. Like a shark, you have to keep swimming or die. Pam's all too aware there's a well-shod, superbly coiffed army of bright young things waiting in the wings, ready to pounce and take her spot in front of the cameras should she even break a nail.

So when an opportunity came up to be weekend anchor, Pam snapped it up. The woman who was anchoring the weekend shows had been tapped to go to the United States. Pam was offered the spot. Naturally she said, "I'll take it." It was perfect, really.

We were home together during the week, learning the ropes, with Nicholas up every couple of hours at night, but Pam still had her foot in the door at work. She anchored the six o'clock news and the eleven o'clock news and could come home between shifts, her nipples oozing milk— sometimes her shirts, under her suits, would be soaked—to breast-feed Nick.

But then, after a while, she went back to work full-time, and Nicholas and I were left staring at each other, wondering, I think, What do I do now? What do you do with a creature who doesn't walk or talk or even sit up by himself?

It was a warm spring. All I could think of, at first, was to take him on long, long walks, with a bottle of "express milk" (milk pumped from Pam's breasts by means of a primitive hand pump) and a change of diaper. These walks would last five, six, seven hours at a stretch, shamelessly killing time. From the stroller, all swaddled in blankets, Nick would stare up at me, with his little baby-blue marbles. After a while, he would fall asleep. Then he'd wake up, then fall asleep again.

Has anyone spent more time walking than I did in those first few months? I doubt it—unless there's some tramp who spends his whole day walking. But they mostly seem to lie or stagger around.

I didn't know what else to do with him. I couldn't sit in the house all day—that would be madness. I needed help, but where do you find that? How does one go about finding a nanny?

One day I gave a reading of *Chump Change* for a group called MOMS, which stood for Mornings Out Means Socializing. These MOMS met every Tuesday morning at a church in one of the wealthier neighbourhoods of town, to listen to readings or lectures or whatever, while a cadre of crack nannies looked after their kids in the basement.

Nick and I had to take two buses to get there. He stared wide-eyed and sucked on his pacifier or drank from his bottle the whole way. When we arrived at the church, my contact person took me down to the basement. This was my first glimpse at a daycare-like scenario. The room was filled with babies: babies in car seats, babies in strollers, babies crawling on the floor, babies sleeping in cribs against the wall. It looked like there were about thirty babies, all being looked after by six almost identical-looking white-haired women.

"I'm here to give a reading," I said to the nanny nearest me. She was pushing a baby back and forth in a stroller with one hand and rocking another baby in a car seat with her foot. "They said I could leave Nicholas with you."

"She'll help you," she said, motioning towards another nanny with her free hand. The other nanny took me in hand, wrote Nicholas on a piece of masking tape and stuck it to his bottle. I said goodbye to him and went upstairs. This was the first time he'd ever been in a room that didn't also have Pam or me in it. I hoped he would be OK.

The MOMS were the best audience I ever had (the worst was a class of high-school students who sat there like an oil painting the whole time, barely cracking a smile). Raucous, rowdy, heckling, they were almost out of control. Mostly I think they were just happy to get out of the house, to be able to hang around with each other while someone else looked after their kids. Everything else was gravy.

After the reading, they asked the usual questions. How autobiographical is it? ("Completely.") Do you write every day? ("Yes.") How does one go about getting published? ("Write a great manuscript.") When they ran out of questions, I said, "Listen, ladies, I have a question for *you*. My wife went back to work, and I'm looking after my son, Nicholas, full-time now—"

"I know! We heard! That's great!" several MOMS yelled out.

"Thanks," I said. "But I have to admit I don't really have a clue what to do with him all day. . . ."

"No one does!" someone called out. They all laughed. "What *do* you do with him?" another one yelled out.

"To tell you the truth, I take him on these really long walks—"

"That's good for him at that age!"

"That's what he needs right now!"

"But I'm talking about really, *really* long walks, ladies, like five- or six- or seven-hour walks. I bring his bottle, some baby goo and diapers, and we just walk all over the city. He falls asleep and wakes up in his stroller. I don't know what else to do with him. He doesn't walk; he doesn't crawl; he can't even sit up by himself. I can't just hold onto him all day—I'd go crazy. But I've been thinking lately that I need someone to come in part-time, a few hours a couple days a week, and I don't know where to start looking."

They gave me a couple of suggestions: look on the bulletin board of your local drop-in centre, also community centres and ask around. I, in turn, gave one of the MOMS my phone number, and she said she'd pin it up on a bulletin board.

As it turned out, though, I didn't have to pursue any of those avenues. After the meeting broke up, and everyone was getting their coats together, a little white-haired lady materialized out of the crowd and introduced herself as Audrey. She turned out to be one of the downstairs nannies.

"Someone told me you were looking for someone to look after Nicholas. I could come to you Mondays and Wednesdays, if you like."

I have to admit, it was an odd feeling at first to hand my kid over to a total stranger. I'm even nervous when it comes to handing him over to my mother. (She seems so absent-minded lately. "Be careful crossing the street," I tell her, the last thirty years of life having come full circle.) The first time Audrey pushed him down the street and around the corner, I thought, I have no paperwork on this woman. I don't even know where she lives. What if she never comes back? But she was approved by MOMS, wasn't she? They must have all the usual recommendations, right?

That first year of looking after Nicholas is pretty much a blur, I have to admit. My hat's off to women like Louise Erdrich and Anne Lamott who wrote poignant, thoughtful journals on their first-borns' first year. For the first year of Nicholas's life, all my diary entries would have been pretty much the same:

Octoberish

Nothing happened today. I bought some broccoli.
Lord, I'm tired.

I was so tired all the time. In the beginning I thought I
could write while he napped—women chuckle at that notion. After being up three, four, five times a night, I would
run, not walk, to the couch while he napped, to have a nap
of my own. Or if we were out on a walk and he fell asleep, I
would immediately turn the wheels of the stroller towards
home. I was a snooze-missile, zeroing in on my target. I've
always been very pro-nap. I've never had any guilt about
naps. But during the first year of Nicholas's life, my whole
day was organized around them. As a headline in a parenting magazine I managed to glance at put it: "Nap Time:
Your Window to Sanity."

It seemed I started aging at triple the normal rate. In
ten years, I'll be a senior citizen! Ten years after that, I'll
be on my last legs! Clothes-wise, I've always affected an
ironic oldster look: cardigans, baggy cuffed pants, little
granny glasses, clothes that seem to say, "Obviously I'm
too young to wear all this stuff." Lamb dressed as mutton.
Now, though, with a burgeoning gut and joints that
crackle and pop like chestnuts roasting over an open fire
every time I rise from my chair, I'm not so sure how
"ironic" it all is.

At some point during that year, in a last-ditch bid to
salvage some sort of glamour for myself, I dyed my hair
silvery grey—or "mother-of-pearl," as my stylist, Dean,
calls it. One day, pulling up to the house, my mother said,

"Oh, Dave, that's funny, when I saw you from the back, I thought it was your father."

Oh, great, I thought. One of these days I'll be walking down the street and someone will say, "Hey, Professor Eddie, what's happening? How's your son Dave?"

"I *am* Dave, you fool," I'll say, shaking my cane at them.

All in all, I'm pleased with the hair, though. I get a lot of compliments, like "You look sort of Silver-Surfer-ish" and "You look like you're from the future."

"I *am* from the future," I respond conspiratorially. "What nobody needs to know is I had to come back because I couldn't afford it."

That first year was a tough one, a blinding blur of sleeplessness, diapers and baby goo (our cat's life went straight downhill, too—but it was too cushy, anyway). At the end of it, as if our lives weren't stressful enough, we went on our honeymoon—a honeymoon that almost broke us, that might have cracked a lesser couple.

6. OUR HORRIBLE

HONEYMOON

"I hate you." "You're an asshole." "I'm not enjoying our relationship right now."

That's just a little sampler-pak of some of the things Pam said to me during the course of our horrible honeymoon.

Obviously I wouldn't mention any of this if our relationship weren't, for the most part, peaceful, mutually respectful, loving and even passionate. However, as Nora Ephron says, having a baby is "like dropping a hand grenade in a marriage." I think some of that was in effect on our honeymoon, although personally, I prefer to draw my metaphor from the world of finance. Our honeymoon was an "adjustment," in the same way stock markets experience periodic adjustments, in order to bring them more into line with reality. Until that point, we'd been living under the aegis of a cheerful illusion: either of us would love to take Nicholas, our beautiful new baby boy, whenever we could, all the time. "Oh, you'd like me to take him? Certainly, of course, I'd love to!" In the course of our disastrous, star-crossed honeymoon, though, that changed to "Why don't you take him—and *go away*?"

We got married when Pam was five months pregnant and had to wear a dress with an empire waist. The original plan was to do our honeymoon in two parts, or phases. Phase I: a week at Max's cottage, where, if you recall, Pam and I first proclaimed our love for one another. Phase II: two weeks in Vancouver, British Columbia, and environs, where Pam grew up and her best friend Julie now lived.

Unfortunately, though, we had to postpone Phase II. I had a bit of an accident. I cut my foot, carved it up like a Christmas turkey. Like an idiot, I was walking around in my bare feet when I kicked over a glass that some fool (me) had left lying on the dock. It landed on its side, broke in half, then rolled over onto its base, just as my bare foot came down on the jagged edge.

"OW!" I said, falling back into a lawn chair. Blood was spurting everywhere. Max mopped it up with a towel. Then we drove to the hospital for stitches—and if you're ever feeling invincible, try having a baby-faced intern who looks like he should be in high school put twelve stitches in your foot with a huge, curved needle and insufficient anaesthetic. Then we'll see how tough you are. Well, maybe it wouldn't bother you, but I, wimpy househusband that I am, whimpered, cried out and nearly burst into tears of pain and cowardice. I left the hospital feeling like an old man. It was a grim glimpse into the far future. Pam pushed me out of the hospital in a wheelchair; Max and Julie walked sombrely beside me. Then we drove to the pharmacy to buy me a cane. I could barely walk. The rest of the honeymoon was off.

We didn't get to Vancouver until the next summer, by which time Nicholas was already ten months old. And if having a kid is like dropping a hand grenade into a marriage, then travelling with a kid is like being carpet-bombed.

The stress began on the plane. I can't believe airlines' fly-by-the-seat-of-their-pants policy towards babies. It can be summed up as "Hold them on your lap for the whole flight." How realistic is that? The weekend before, there'd been a piece on the television program 20/20 about parents who let go of their kids during heavy turbulence. The kids were injured, and the parents felt guilty, thinking, "I should have been able to hold on." But the point of the piece was it's impossible *not* to let go of your kid during heavy turbulence.

Luckily we were in business class (the flight was a wedding present from my friend Brian, using his frequent-flyer points), and Nicholas could crawl around a bit. A little girl about his age was also on the flight, and she and Nicholas played with toys and books on the floor until the flight attendant came over and told us we had to pick the kids up and hold onto them.

"The whole flight?" I asked.

"Don't you realize that if we encounter any turbulence he could be seriously injured?" he said, quite nastily.

"Do you have any children of your own?" I asked him, equally nastily.

"Pardon me?"

"I said, 'Do you have any children of your own?'"

"No—"

"So you have no idea what's involved—"

"Excuse me, sir, but that's not true. I spend a lot of time with my nephews and nieces—"

"Well then you know how unrealistic it is to be expected to hold a kid on your lap for six hours."

"Well, it's airline policy, sir. I'm sorry."

Airline policy it might be, and I'm not sure what my solution would be—some car-seat-like device, perhaps, or maybe even a little fenced-off play area. I don't know. I'm not an engineer. I don't even have a job! Let the airlines hold a bunch of meetings and come up with a solution. If they can get a ten-ton bucket of bolts in the air via a series of controlled explosions, they can figure out a way to accommodate children in the cabin.

The stress didn't end with the flight, either. As women have known since the dawn of time, a vacation with a very young child isn't a vacation at all. In fact, it's worse, really, because you don't have your usual support system in effect: no nannies, grannies, friends or family, and no dishwasher. As Rae André puts it in *Homemakers: The Forgotten Workers*, "The idea of a homemaker taking a vacation is usually more fantasy than reality. Often for her the family vacation is simply more of the same—cooking, picking up, watching the children. In reality, going to work in an office would be more of a change."

I'm not saying I did all the "family work" on our vacation. The problem in retrospect, I think, was lack of a schedule. We never knew who was supposed to be taking Nicholas when. We worked on a strictly ad hoc, volunteer basis. Could you take him? Do you want me to take him?

Should I change his diaper? Do you want to put him to bed? At home, because of Pam's work schedule, our lives naturally fell into a routine, a pattern. On our honeymoon, we were all at sea.

And I'm not saying Nicholas was bad. From birth, he's been (for the most part) an outstandingly good-natured and even-tempered kid. He was born cool, and he stayed cool. But on our honeymoon, he started doing something new. The moment you stopped anywhere for more than a minute, he started squirming and fussing and pointing and urging us onward, onward. Let's go, pronto. What're we hanging around here for? What's happening? Let's get a move on. What's next on the agenda? We couldn't sit down for a cup of coffee, let alone have a poignant candlelit dinner.

On top of that, we were doing the honeymoon on the cheap, staying at Julie's. Pam, Nicholas and I were all staying on top of each other in Julie's living room, with the curtain always drawn because it was on the ground floor. We would be crammed, knees touching, around her tiny kitchen table, begging Nicholas to eat just one tiny spoonful of mush, while he screamed and kicked and pointed to things he wanted.

Pam and I turned on each other like a couple of caged lab rats. The worst part of it was we were always trying *not* to argue in front of Julie. I hate it when couples air their dirty laundry in public. It makes me really uncomfortable, and the only thing worse than witnessing a couple openly bickering in public is being part of that couple. But on this honeymoon, Pam was so steamed at me all the time, it seemed, she couldn't help but let the odd tart remark slip in front of Julie—which never failed to send me into a frenzy.

"Don't you *dare*," I'd say later, pushing the stroller across the street. We went on walks to argue. We argued while walking up and down the streets of Julie's neighbour-hood, taking turns pushing the stroller; we argued in parks, taking turns pushing Nick on the swing. "Never, ever speak to me like that in front of anyone *again*."

"Don't tell me what to do!" Pam would retort, with equal vehemence. It was a Mexican standoff. Although I'm almost always wrong about everything, that doesn't stop me from being extremely bossy; but Pam refuses with maximum indignation to be bossed around by me. In an earlier era of human history, Pam, perhaps, would have bowed before my imperious, unilateral edicts. But now, who says who bosses who? She makes the money—and it's a credit to Pam that never, not once in any of our acrimonious arguments has she ever said, "Shut up! Fuck you! *I pay for everything!*" She must have been tempted, at times. I don't know if I would have been able to show such forbearance in her shoes.

It had been a while since Pam and Julie had seen each other; so naturally they wanted some tête-à-tête time, her-mana a hermana. That's where "Why don't you take him— and *go away*" came in. Pam was always suggesting I take Nicholas for walks, or run errands (even on honeymoons there are errands) and take him. Oops, we're out of coffee. Dave, why don't you get some lattes—and take Nicholas.

Pam disputes this, but I remember a lot of long, long walks, just me and Nicholas, me muttering to him, "It's like *they're* on honeymoon, and I'm their nanny. Who do they think they are? Who do they think *I* am? They can't treat me like this!" Nicholas and I killed time; I deliberately stayed away for longer than I had to, to see if they'd missed me, but they never did. Pam missed Nick a bit, but she and Julie would be laughing or having a great talk or otherwise completely enraptured with one another. But it was *our* honeymoon! Once, to try to have some sort of fun, I took Nicholas to a bar. He slept in his stroller at my feet while I moodily consumed two beers and read the local alternative weekly. But the beer tasted bitter, like gall and wormwood, and the paper was boring, and after about an hour, I pushed him home.

The worst fights Pam and I had were not the ones where she said, "You take him—and go away." The worst ones were the ones where I said, "I'm taking him," and she said, "Oh no you're not. I am!" Both of us shaking with anger—like a miniature custody battle. I can't imagine what it would be like to be involved in a real custody battle. It must be awful.

Where did all this bad energy come from? Probably me. Our lousy honeymoon was probably my fault, like everything else. I like to work. I've never known what to do on vacations. On vacations, I feel the lack of a life work, like life's too short and chaos is descending. On vacations, all the energy I usually pour into writing goes into arguing, chewing people out and brooding over the world's injustice to Me and indifference to my problems. Whereas when I'm writing, you could bounce ping-pong balls off my head, and I wouldn't get mad at you.

My parents dragged me all over the world, sightseeing, when I was a kid, and the whole exercise struck me as a gigantic pointless bore. To quote Lao-tzu: "the farther one goes, the less one knows." You bring yourself wherever you go. We dragged our squabbling family all over the world, sullying the world's great sights. We should have stayed home, reading books, with ashes on our foreheads, learning silence and humility. Then we could gawk at the Taj Mahal or Michelangelo's *David*.

For me, the idiocy of tourism was summed up in a single vignette from our horrible honeymoon. We were driving on a little road that goes around Stanley Park in Vancouver, going along at a snail's pace behind a minivan, sightseeing. Julie, our tour guide, was telling us all about Skana the killer whale, who was housed at the aquarium in Stanley Park, but had become so bored in captivity, she committed suicide by repeatedly bonking her head against the side of the pool. She hemorrhaged and died. There was a short silence as each of us absorbed the implications of that unusual act. Suddenly, to our left, on the emerald green lawn of Stanley Park, a polka band struck up. And slowly, from a side window of the minivan in front of us, the lens of a video camera peeked out, trained on the polka band. The van didn't slow down or stop. After the invisible occupant decided he or she had enough footage, the lens withdrew.

That lens said it all to me. Travel and tourism were founded in the spirit of adventure, weren't they? But our atavistic, untamed love of adventure has come to this: a video lens peeking out of a minivan, aimed at a polka band.

In the spirit of adventure, Julie, Pam and I took the ferry to Vancouver Island and drove to Tofino, on the west coast, where a friend of Julie's had a place we could stay in free. Tofino was a tourist trap, but we heard from a couple of local yokels about a little stretch of beach almost no one knew about. And truly it was exquisite, about half a mile long, surrounded by trees, with numerous little spots to camp and make a fire, and only a half-dozen other people.

An ideal, idyllic place for swimming and relaxing; however, I was far from relaxed. On the way to the beach, in the car, Pam and Julie were discussing a "cute guy" in my presence. That was an indignity Pam had never subjected me to before. Sitting in the back seat with Nicholas, I thought, What am I, a eunuch? I've always made it a point to never talk about women I find attractive in front of her. So far, she'd accorded me the same courtesy. What had changed?

At the beach, we lay down on towels and relaxed; but then Nicholas started fussing. I martyrishly offered to take him to the other end of the beach, so he wouldn't bother the girls. I was half joking, I think, but the girls didn't hesitate to take me up on it. While I was getting him ready, Pam said, also half jokingly, I guess (and I quote from my diary entry): "Hurry up and get him out of here!" The reason I was taking so long? I, Cinderfella, was changing his diaper.

I stormed off to the other end of the beach. How could she, the woman to whom I'd been married only a year and who had borne my child, be so callous, cruel and rude?

It may sound strange to say, but I found myself yearning for masculine society on my honeymoon, to get as far away as I could from endless discussions of: Do you think I'm fat? No, honey, you're *perfect*. Seriously, I am becoming a little fat, don't you think? No, no, etc. And God help anyone who says, "You know what? You could stand to lose a couple of pounds." I longed to sit around with someone like Max, who might poke me in my paunch, his finger sinking deep into my flabby rolls, and say, "What's that? Are you giving birth to a little baby six-pack?"

The next day, we went to visit another beach, a popular tourist destination. A heavy fog hung over the whole beach, though, and you couldn't see anything. After a while the girls, bored, decided to go into town to do some shopping. I hate shopping with other people, plus I wanted to be alone, so I said, "You know what? Why don't you leave me here, go shopping and come back when you're finished?"

They protested feebly, but were probably glad to get rid of me. I think Pam wanted me to take Nicholas so she could shop unfettered with Julie, but I made it clear I wanted to be alone.

I walked along the beach a ways, past people emerging from and then disappearing into the mist, until I came upon a little hill with a path that led up to a weather station. The weather station was locked, but I sat on the porch to ruminate and collect my thoughts. The sea was calm, the surf smooth, quiet and soothing (I guess that's why they call it the Pacific), but I was seething. We hadn't had sex once during our whole quarrelsome honeymoon. Perhaps she was losing interest in me? Maybe one day she'd have an affair with a cute guy and even wind up leaving me for him?

I became so upset, I even drew a sketch in my notebook, a bird's-eye view of the room I would rent after we split up. With my pencil and eraser, I arranged and rearranged my few meagre items of furniture. Let's see, I'd put the desk here, my chair here, my trunk here—no, over there. It could serve as a footstool/coffee table. And, of course, I'd have to buy a bed and put that somewhere—or maybe another cot. My mother probably had my old cot in her basement. I'd sleep on that. I'd get a lot of work done, do push-ups and sit-ups in the morning, live like a convict or soldier.

But where would you get the money to rent this room? I asked myself. If Pam dumped me, how would I live? I couldn't try to soak her for alimony; that would be dishonourable. Anyway, after the judge found out Pam had patiently and uncomplainingly supported me while I wrote my first novel, he'd laugh me out of court. She'd probably win custody of Nicholas, too. Women win custody in something like 96 percent of cases. Judges simply assume men can't look after kids. In my case, the judge might have cause for reflection when I tell him I stayed home with Nicholas, but how would I even afford a law-yer? She'd win custody, and then perhaps I, the faceless drudge who had nowhere else to go, would wind up living in a wing of her house, forced to babysit while she went out with a succession of "cute guys."

These were my thoughts as I sat on the porch of that locked-up weather station, scribbling in my notebook, soupy fog all around me; and I felt, I think, for the first time something of the terrible powerlessness and helplessness that women must have felt through the centuries.

Later that day, though, I had an experience that restored my faith that I was, if not strong, if not a survivor, then at least incredibly persistent and stubborn and would probably be fine over the long haul. A minor and mundane incident, perhaps, but it was no accident, I think, that it concerned the *barbecue*, a nexus of so many contradictory symbols, both masculine and feminine: fire and meat (man), but also cooking (woman); the Promethean conquest of nature and subsequent blind pursuit of technology and weaponry, but also the hearth, which belongs to the sphere of home and family.

Something was wrong with the fucking coals. I kept dousing them with lighter fluid and torching them, dousing and torching, but they wouldn't light. Now I know, gentlemen, you will immediately begin vying with one another to tell me I should have waited a few minutes to let the lighter fluid soak in; but I did that, and still nothing happened. I'm telling you, the coals were stale or something. Finally, I'd used up the entire bottle, and I'd only lit one corner of one coal. I picked up the coal between thumb and forefinger, sat down in a lawn chair and started blowing on the lit part, refusing to give up. The girls pronounced the sight of me ludicrous and went into the cottage, chuckling to themselves and saying, "I guess we're cooking on the stove tonight."

Twenty minutes later, we were grilling steaks on a bed of glowing coals. Ha! I thought. That'll show them. I am a man, I said to myself, as the steaks sizzled and spat on the Hibachi. And not only a man but a *Capricorn*, stubborn, persistent, plodding but determined as hell. Maybe I'll have a hard time in the short run, but can success be denied me in the long run?

Laugh at me if you will, but after the incident with the coals I felt calmer, more secure, more centred. That night, Pam and I had sex, became a loving couple again, and only bickered once or twice after that. It's even possible our whole, horrible honeymoon was, once again, all my fault, that a great deal of what I'd been thinking and feeling during the last week or so was due to hypersensitivity on my part, as Pam claims. It's true we househusbands are a touchy bunch, "touchy as a hunchback," as they say, or used to, in Russia.

These days, when we travel, Pam and I are like a crack team of Swiss paratroopers or U.S. Navy SEALS. On our most recent trip to Max's cottage, for example, the other guests laughed at our watch-synchronizing, clock-punching ways. Pam even gave me a hard time once when I was ten minutes late to take over Nicholas. She pointed to her watch, to everyone's bemusement and mock horror, saying, "Dave, you're ten minutes late." She was wearing her swimsuit and had a towel wrapped around her shoulders. And I would've done the same if she'd been late.

The point is not so much that each of us has to be looking after him for a certain amount of time. It's that both of us know, at any given time, which of us is responsible for him, whose watch it is. This cuts down on confusion, which leads to psychological wear and tear. So if we're all on the dock, and it's Pam's watch, and Nicholas tears off at a dead run for the end of the dock, looking like he's going to throw himself headfirst into the lake, sink like a stone and drown, I just yawn, and sip my gin and tonic. She takes off after him. Because it's *her problem*, see?

In practice, this system works better for me than it does for her. If it's my watch and he takes off, she's more likely to scream, "Dave! Aren't you going to run after him?" But she doesn't have to, as I'm always explaining to her. If it's my watch, it's my problem and I'm responsible. Absurd as it may seem to others, this system has cut down on the aggregate number of arguments we've had on vacations. It's when there's confusion over who should be looking after him at any given moment that we run into real problems.

Before you have a kid, your life is basically all leisure; afterwards it's basically all work. As long as you realize this, you'll be fine. That, and your days of freedom are over. I'm not talking about the freedom to jump on a plane and have brunch in Burkina Faso or a picturesque weekend in a

Paris pied-à-terre, but the freedom to go on a bike ride or to a coffee shop to meet a friend, simply to sail out the front door without a second thought. With Nicholas, just getting to the corner store (especially in the middle of winter) can be a titanic battle, complete with tears, laughter, raised voices, tender reconciliations, negotiations, whispered promises and wrestling matches. Getting a carton of milk can be like one of the twelve labours of Hercules, and every day I pray to El Niño for a short winter.

For your relationship to work, you have to learn to work together. Pam's always been very worky; now I'm worky, too. We're quite a worky couple, and if one of us isn't working at any given moment that person feels guilty before the other and has to explain and justify. That's why our relationship works, I think: because we work together on various projects. We don't have time to argue.

I'm trying to learn how to *putter*. The solution to many of my problems lies in the realm of puttering, I believe. Constant, low-level work, puttering exists somewhere in the grey area between work and rest, between motivation and inertia. That's the ticket, I think. You don't wear yourself out, you don't get frazzled, but you get things done. The major religions seem to have little to say about puttering but, as far as I can tell, as long as you are doing something—like a monk plaiting palm leaves—your soul will be at peace.

And if there's one thing I've learned from observing Nicholas, it's how much of human behaviour is attributable to the state of the organism. When you're tired/sick/hungry, you become cranky and enter into confrontations with those around you. This applies not only to infants, toddlers and older children, but adults as well. Don't argue when you're tired. Wait until you've had a good night's rest—and since that never happens, you'll never argue.

Also, don't argue when you're drunk. In general, I'm very pro-booze, though of course I believe in everything in moderation (including moderation itself; you don't want to overdo *that*). But just as you shouldn't drink and drive, you shouldn't drink and argue. Your judgment is impaired; your reflexes are all wrong; you don't hit the brakes quickly enough. In fact, couples should probably have a home Breathalyzer, and if you're over the legal limit to drive you should also eschew chewing each other out.

And—maybe it's having an agent, negotiating book contracts, but these days everything looks like a negotiation to me. You have your position; other people have theirs; you try to negotiate your way to some sort of middle ground. This is as true of our personal lives as it is of our professional lives, but whereas in the professional sphere negotiations are mostly about money, in our marriage the negotiations are mostly about time. Every hour of our week is as heavily negotiated as a professional athlete's endorsement contracts: when she puts him down, when I wake him up, what days she gets to sleep in (Sundays), what days I get to sleep in (Saturdays) and so on. Friday afternoons, from four to seven, is Family Fun Time. In order to get extra time for this book, I had to promise Pam "a month of Sundays," no less than thirty extra sleep-in days, each of which will no doubt age me a month.

And it helps, I find, to remember that, at bottom, Pam and I are just socializing. "We're just socializing," I tell myself (sometimes through gritted teeth). Marriage is a very deep, complex and intimate form of socializing, but it's still socializing: the same protocols and strictures are still in effect. It helps to mind your p's and q's, to be courteous, gentlemanly and gentlewomanly. Someday I'd like to write a book called *Manners for Marriages*, all about how to behave decently to your spouse. I'm amazed at the number of people who seem just to pull the rip cord when they get married, becoming unattractive, abusive, boorish, offensive—not their best selves, by a long chalk. Which is odd, when you consider that you could get hit by a bus, and it's probably your spouse who will deliver the eulogy. It behooves you to be on the best behaviour you can manage at all times.

Also, as any parenting book or pamphlet will tell you, you need to make time for each other. Hire a sitter and go out, as often as you can afford it. What you hear less often, but is equally important, I think, is to remember everyone needs a certain amount of time to themselves, to *be* themselves. Personally, I need a good two to three hours a day to myself in order to feel human.

It's true having Nicholas around does put a certain strain on our lives. He puts pressure on everything. With Nick on the scene, there's no turning back—no looking back, even. We're strapped in now, our harnesses snapped into place and double-checked by the attendant; all we can do now is clutch the safety bar with white-knuckled hands and hang on for our lives.

7. THE HONG KONG HANDOVER

Most of the time, Pam and I get along extremely well, and our little experiment in gender-bending is a success.

I'm still very ambitious. And that's something you'll find most househusbands would like you to know right off the top: we work not only in the home, but from it, as well. It's all a question of efficiency, and I've recently acquired both a fax machine and an agent in order to pester the world more efficiently. I've always been a major-league procrastinator, a subscriber to the notion that "writing begins with a thorough cleanup of your office," not to mention ironing shirts, alphabetizing your library, etc. As a bachelor, it was not unusual for me to procrastinate for *seven hours* before settling down to write my first line of the day. Now, though, I might just iron a single shirt, make a phone call, type a letter, grab some coffee and get cracking after only an hour or two.

May I say, though, I also enjoy my in-house duties? Is that too odd? I love to cook—and I use the term "cook" in perhaps a different sense than men of my father's generation do. I remember the blue-moon occasions when my father used to cook when I was a kid. He always made a big deal about it: "Gather around, children, and observe as I actually place the cheese and onions *inside* the hamburger!"

"Yeah, yeah, Dad," we'd think. "They're *burgers*: slap 'em on the grill and pony 'em up pronto, like Mom always does."

I make all the meals. I am the "primary provender provider" of our family, if I may coin a faux politically correct term. If I don't cook, we don't eat, or else we order pizza. Well, that's probably not quite fair. In a pinch, Pam will rush out to the grocery store, grab a hunk of meat, heave it into the oven along with a couple of spuds, and boil a pot of green beans on the stove for her specialty, green beans amandine. However, in practice, I'm the one who shops, plans and pores over cookbooks. I've always enjoyed food; now a significant portion of my life is devoted to it. My first thought upon waking these days is often, Wonder what we'll have for dinner tonight? (Definitely a step up from bachelor days, when it might be, Who's this?)

But by far, the best and most important part of my job is, obviously, looking after Nicholas. It may sound odd to say, but I look upon taking care of him as a crucial step in my spiritual path, in my development as a human being, "The Child is father of the Man," Wordsworth wrote, and it's definitely true in my case. Who would have thought a baby could teach an adult lessons of patience, tolerance and forbearance? But so he has. "He has such wise eyes," people will say when I stroller him into a store or café.

"Yes, he's a philosopher," I invariably respond. And his philosophy is "Life's great." Everything that happens is wonderful. He sneezes and smiles. Sneezing is fun! A dog licks his face and he laughs. Dogs are great!

His philosophy is starting to rub off on me. Staying home with Nicholas is not how I imagined my life turning out, but in some ways it's probably better than the fate I would have designed for myself, with the limos, hot tubs and Vassar girls. Proof positive, once again, of the wisdom of Epictetus's dictum "I am always content with that which happens; for I think that what God chooses is better than what I choose." To put it another way, God saved me from the cheeseball I wanted to become. Now I wouldn't trade a day with Nicholas for a sea of hot tubs, for a hot *ocean* full of Vassar girls.

It's a good deal for Pam, too. She gets to keep her fancy-pants career, and who's looking after her child during his prime learning years, at the peak of which, according to the books, he'll learn a new word *every hour*? A wordsmith, if I say so myself, a bookworm, a man in love with the English language since adolescence. Forgive a blunt observation, but at the park where I bring Nicholas in the afternoon, there are usually a half-dozen Filipina nannies sitting on the park benches, chatting among themselves while their little charges play at their feet or race off into the middle distance, and it wouldn't come as a surprise to me if they learned Tagalog before they learned English.

Pam can accept last-minute dinner invitations without frantic phoning. We can go on vacations together and have a modicum of fun, because we spell each other off. She can travel by herself without experiencing "runway guilt," because she knows Nick's with a relative. Recently she went on a shopping trip to New York with two of her fellow anchors, both women. She spent the whole time trying on shoes, having drinks and brunch and checking out suits and hardly thought about him at all. I'm proud of that fact.

So, it's a good deal for me, it's a good deal for Pam. Hmmm, let me see . . . am I forgetting anyone?

Oh, yes, it's a good deal for Nicholas, too—or so I flatter myself, anyway. There's no doubt life with Dad is a tad more . . . rough and tumble than it might be with Mom. We call it "the Hong Kong Handover" when Pam hands Nicholas over to me for the day. He goes from the relatively decent civilized world of Mom's rule to the backwards, corrupt banana republic of Dad's regime. I've often pictured Nicholas writing *his* memoirs, *Daddy Direst* (which he'll probably publish to international acclaim at age nineteen): "I grew up in the shadow of an insane asylum. Since my mother was the primary breadwinner of the family, I was left to the tender mercies of my father, who took me to numerous bars, dipped my pacifier in his beer, and allowed me to gnaw on the celery sticks of his Bloody Marys. He never changed my diaper until it was as heavy as a sack of hammers. My first daycare centre was a lingerie store. While other kids were playing with learning toys in a stimulating environment, I was playing peekaboo with a lingerie saleswoman, darting behind the bra-and-panties-clad mannequins. . . ."

All true, I'm afraid. I often take Nicholas to my local, Squirly's, dip his pacifier in my beer, and/or allow him to gnaw on the garnish of my cocktail. "Hey, they do it all the time in Europe," I say whenever one of these parenting techniques draws an incredulous stare, though in truth I have no idea. Last time I was in Europe I was nineteen, too busy sleeping in phone booths and getting high in hash bars to notice much about their parenting techniques. I have a feeling the Europe I'm thinking of, where parents are much more lax, louche and laid-back, where they feed their kids wine for lunch, dinner and maybe even breakfast, is largely a Europe of my imagination. Perhaps it would be more accurate to say, "Hey, they did this all the time in medieval Europe!"

But Nicholas seems to like bars. There's lots of room to crawl around ("That was me Friday night," I overheard one patron say once when Nicholas windmilled by in his patented stiff-legged style). And he gets plenty of attention. The waitresses all love him, pick him up, jounce him on their hips and fashion little toys for him out of swizzle sticks, maraschino cherries, olives and cocktail onions.

One day, my favourite bartender, Liz, inherited some money and opened a lingerie store, Nearly Naked, just down the street, right on my stroller route. Naturally I would pop in to say "Hi" whenever I passed. Once, when I didn't, she said sarcastically, "I saw you go by yesterday with Nicholas. But I guess you were *too busy* to stop in."

"OK, I'll stop in more often," I said evenly. "But don't stare directly into his cuteness rays for too long, or you may become zombified. You will walk the earth muttering to yourself, 'Coochy-coochy, he's such a cutie,' your ovaries will begin to hum 'The Battle Hymn of the Republic,' and your will will no longer be your own!"

Thus I tried to warn her, but did she listen? One day as

she was playing with him on the floor, she looked up at me with pinwheel eyes.

"Why don't you leave him here? I'll look after him. You ... shop or something," she said, making a shooing motion with her hands, as if sweeping me out of the store.

At first I demurred, but she insisted, and finally I accepted. And that's how Nearly Naked became Nicholas's first daycare centre. From time to time, I drop him off there and head out to do errands and shopping while Liz looks after him for an hour. I tell myself that Nearly Naked is, after all, a "stimulating" environment. There's an old-fashioned barber chair, with a foot pedal that makes it go up and down. Nicholas loves to ride on it, while Liz or I pump the pedal and say, "First floor, ladies' lingerie. Going up! Second floor, men's haberdashery ... " He laughs and claps his hands. There's also an antique adding machine that makes a satisfying ka-ching sound when Nicholas pulls the lever. Since the clientele is almost exclusively women, Nicholas gets plenty of attention and coochy-coochy action. And he increases sales; I'm sure of it. Women look at him and think, "Maybe if I get a really sexy bra my lover will give me one of *those*." Perhaps, looking at Nicholas, they even tell themselves that cheap lingerie is the ultimate false economy, I don't know.

And of course it's far from unpleasant for me to lounge on the scallop-shaped, crushed-velvet loveseat against the wall, flipping through *The History of Underwear* and other lingerie-centric publications and discussing cleavage strategies and other matters of extreme pith and importance with Liz's customers. And if I'm happy, Nicholas is happy, right? Babies pick up on vibes, which is why you have to look after yourself first and foremost. It's like when you're on a plane and you suddenly lose cabin pressure (that's probably as good an analogy for parenthood as I can think of: A sudden loss of cabin pressure). You have to put the oxygen mask over *your* mouth first; *then* you look after your child.

Or maybe that's all just cheap rationalization and I'm nothing more than an old-fashioned Bad Dad. What if I'm not doing Nicholas any favours by staying home with him, bleeding the family finances white, allowing my mind to turn to mush and my body into a pear? What if I'm actually doing him a *disservice*? Why don't I abandon this crazy gender-bending experiment already, get a job and leave the care and feeding of Nicholas to a team of trained professionals?

These doubts, fears and guilt came to a head when Nicholas was about ten months old. Around that time, I noticed that whenever Nicholas and I were strollering in the park and he saw another kid, he'd yell, clap, do a fake cough—anything to get the other kid's attention. Suddenly it occurred to me: *he's* bored; *he's* lonely; *he's* tired of hanging around with *me* and would prefer to be with his age-mates. Could this be a taste of the future?

By sinister coincidence, one of the best daycare centres in the city, by universal parental acclamation, is located in none other than the mental-health centre across the street. It's out back, in a separate wing, sealed off from all the nutcases—oops, I mean *consumers of mental-health services*. A couple of my friends have their kids there, and sometimes, after dropping them off on the way to their exciting, rewarding careers, they'll stop off here at the house to brag and boast about how stimulated and socialized their kids are at the daycare, how quickly they're learning to talk, etc. One morning, I was picking up my newspaper, still in my bathrobe, when my friend Les walked by. We chatted, me standing on the front porch, clutching a coffee, with the paper under my arm. She told me she'd just dropped her kid, Miles, age one, off at the daycare centre.

"How do you like that daycare, by the way?" I asked, as if casually.

"Oh, it's great," she said. "The staff's really friendly and very well-trained, and they do a great job."

"You know, Les, it's funny, but lately I've been wondering whether I'm not doing Nicholas a *disservice* by staying home with him, that maybe he's bored stiff staying home with me, and he'd be better off in daycare."

"Well, you know, Dave," she said. "I've found that when I'm looking after my kids, I always have another agenda, like shopping or sending a fax. Whereas at the daycare centre, it's all about the kids. It's a very stimulating environment and there are all kinds of learning toys and games—there's even a disco ball in the ceiling."

Learning toys? Disco ball? Meanwhile, behind me, Nicholas—a possible budding Mozart or Bertrand Russell, was playing with pots and pans on the filthy kitchen floor. True, I often have another agenda when I'm strollering him around—in fact, it would be fairer to say I almost always do. Shopping for groceries, running errands, shopping for clothes for *me* (I prance and preen in front of a three-way mirror, while he sits in his stroller sucking on a pacifier, with a look on his face that says, "Dad, don't you realize it's just not *about* you anymore?").

Later that same day, my friend Felicia (of the wedding) came by on her way back from dropping her daughter off at the daycare centre. We had a glass of wine and I told her I was starting to worry that I was boring Nicholas by staying home with him.

"Well, you know, Dave," she said, "they did a study recently that suggests daycare is better than a nanny, because it's more socializing and stimulating."

They did? Our part-time nanny, Audrey, a lifelong caregiving professional, was way better at looking after Nicholas than I was. She knew all the tricks: what ointments and unguents to rub on him (she's a big believer in Vaseline for dry skin and Penaten cream for diaper rash), what medicines to give him, how to trick him into eating his savoury goo when all he wants to eat is his sweet goo, and so on. Likewise, Pam seems imbued with an innate knowledge of exactly what to do with him at all times. For example, she knew by instinct, or osmosis, that before he went to sleep, Nicholas needed to say good night to a family of bears, then stare at his merry-go-round, then watch a little wooden monkey amble down a ramp holding a banana.

None of that ever would have occurred to *me*. I had no instincts for taking care of him. So if Felicia's study was correct, and daycare is better for a kid than a nanny, then the hierarchy probably went like this: 1) Pam, 2) daycare, 3) nanny, 4) Dave.

A couple of days after Felicia's visit, I had a disturbing encounter of a different kind. I was shopping for vegetables in a little variety store that had a narrow entranceway and a cash register near the door. I went in to pay, leaving Nicholas on the sidewalk. He was five feet away from me, in plain sight; but I was in the store and he was on the sidewalk. I was paying for my purchases when a woman stormed in.

"DON'T YOU READ THE PAPERS? I COULD HAVE SNATCHED YOUR BABY!"

"No, you couldn't have!" I said. "I had my eye on him!"

"NO, YOU DIDN'T!"

"Yes, I did!"

"NO, YOU DIDN'T!"

Whew, this bitch has balls, I thought, going toe-to-toe with a huge, unpredictable-looking man like me and pushing the hottest of all hot buttons, the Bad Dad button. She looked like she was about twenty.

"Do *you* have any kids of your own?" I asked her. It's always the childless ones who think they know everything.

"NO, BUT I HAVE NIECES AND NEPHEWS—"

"So you don't really know what you're talking about, do you?"

"I KNOW I WOULD NEVER LEAVE MY KID OUTSIDE A STORE WHILE I WENT INSIDE!"

After a little more discussion in this vein, I wound up giving *her* a suggestion—which she took, actually. As she was leaving, though, she delivered the coup de grâce over her shoulder: "DON'T ABUSE HAVING CHILDREN!"

I *wish* I'd held Nicholas up and said, "Does this child look abused to you?" Nicholas, with his irrefutable nimbus of happiness and health, is my best line of defence against charges of this nature. But I didn't; my reflexes were too slow.

"You know what I love most about being a house-husband and stay-at-home dad?" I asked Pam that night, over dinner.

"What?"

"All the wonderful unsolicited advice you get on the streets."

She looked up from her veal piccata. "Why? What happened?"

Standing up, holding my wineglass, I re-enacted the scene in the vegetable store for Pam's benefit, complete with appropriate grimaces, gestures and gesticulations.

"Hmmm, yes, I can see how that could be annoying," she said, then fell into silence. Uh-oh, I thought. When Pam has something negative to say, she's always silent for a long time, sometimes an incredibly long time, weighing her words and the justice of her forthcoming comments. Even then she's reluctant to speak. I have to *beg* her to criticize me. It's like pulling teeth, and even as I plead with her to tell me what's wrong I know she'll probably be right, as usual. It's agonizing.

"What? What is it? *Please* just tell me what's on your mind. Just blurt it out," I begged her.

"Well, Dave," she said finally. "I really think you should bring him inside when you're shopping."

Damn.

Those encounters with Les, Felicia and the vegetable-store girl, coming on top of each other over the course of a couple of days, really rocked my raison d'être, I can tell you.

As a househusband, far from being an object of contempt, for the first time in my life, I felt helpful, worthwhile, even . . . respectable. In society's eyes, I was transformed from a layabout whose whole goal in life was to do something (write books), which, although certainly a pleasant ornament to the true business of life (making money), no one really needs—something on the level of a tire whitewaller—to a useful, if somewhat gender-bending, contributor to the common weal.

"Society needs househusbands more than it needs writers," a cheeky lawyer had the effrontery to say to me at a party the other day. (I was complaining to him about how hard it is to write when you're looking after a kid.) Society indeed, I thought, sipping my drink—society of philistines. I'd like to change the world so someday it seems eccentric and odd to become a lawyer or banker—and why wouldn't it? What an odd thing to choose to do with your one and only life on this planet.

But what if even as a househusband, I was a stiff, a bum, a patsy, a hack, a palooka? Meanwhile, as a single-income family, we were starting to feel the pinch, living from (Pam's) paycheque to (Pam's) paycheque, slowly sinking like a horse and buggy into a swamp of debt. One day, we reviewed our finances and discovered we didn't have any. Pam's salary covered our day-to-day, week-to-week, month-to-month expenses, but we had no money for contingency, emergency expenses. When you're a homeowner, I've found, especially of a crumbling, decaying old wife-beater's house like ours, everything costs a thousand dollars ("if you're lucky," says my friend Andrew, who had to live in a hotel recently while contractors he was forced to hire by the city ripped apart his house looking for termites he didn't even have). "Say, Pam, the furnace is making a pinging sound; wonder what it is?" We phone the furnace guy, he comes over, heads down to the basement and, after much hushed consultation with his accomplice—oops, I mean apprentice—delivers the verdict: "That pinging sound your furnace is making is . . . a thousand dollars." "Say, Pam, wonder what this pinkish dust is in the bottom of the fireplace?" The chimney guy comes over and, after sitting at the dining-room table with his calculator, surrounded by brochures and a clipboard, renders his judgment: "The pinkish dust in your fireplace is . . . a thousand dollars."

Pam, who as a television news reporter/anchor, could quite reasonably expect to be able to afford the finest of everything, was still driving her old white Suzuki Swift, a car that was more like a golf cart than a car, the same car I pressed her up against after my party for chrome-dome Doug. It was even starting to draw the odd comment from her colleagues in the newsroom, all of whom seemed to drive droptop sports cars or late-model coupes. Not "get a horse" or anything like that, but the sort of gentle teasing that served to let her know "It is still acceptable and possibly even cute that you, an up-and-coming young reporter/anchor, still drive your original bottom-of-the-line car; however, if you continue, you may be hurting your chances for future promotions." That sort of thing is important in television news, as in every other profession. Perception is reality; if you act the part, they give you the part.

And it was all my fault! Where would Pam be if I were a banker, a lawyer . . . or even an environmentalist! The day could conceivably come when she'd decide she missed her chance with the bald environmentalist. By this time, they would have been living in a huge house with solar panels and steaming composter out back, producing only one compressed brick of garbage, the size of a cereal box, a week (with a brood of bald enviro-babies). To our surprise, a couple of our DINK (double-income no kids) acquaintances had snapped up some real snazzy downtown mini-mansions, then hired teams of architects, designers and contractors to renovate them to maximum stylishness. They could actually afford to have certain themes to their houses: Gothic, Spartan, Edwardian or whatever. When we went to dinner parties at their houses, I could see the gleam in Pam's eye, a gleam that said, "I want this." I knew that gleam, of course; she had once turned it on me.

It's hard not to become white trash when you have a kid. You're exhausted and broke; the house is a mess. . . . One day, I'd have to sit Nicholas down and tell him, "Nicholas, you are a poor little white-trash boy. While the other daddies were climbing the ladder as investment bankers, lawyers and record execs, I stayed home with you! I'm sure you're better off for it—psychologically. Unfortunately, though, you now have to work your ass off to get a scholarship."

I became so bent out of shape about these and other equally haunting anxieties that when a job opportunity arose, I lunged for it like a drunken bachelor for the last miniskirted girl in the bar. A company called Shipwreck Films was looking for writers for their hour-long made-for-TV movies about famous marine disasters: the wreck of the *Hesperus*, the *Edmund Fitzgerald*, the *Titanic*. The successful candidate would write the scripts, storyboards and even oversee the filming and, since all the world's antique tankers and frigates are in hot spots like Yalta and Greece, would spend quite a bit of time in those locales. Sounds great, doesn't it? And I had an in, a connection, a foot in the door: someone had recommended me for the job.

Pam was against it, bless her.

"But we need the money, Pam."

"Maybe I could get some voice-over work."

That's Pam all over for you. When money's tight, she doesn't think, "Why doesn't my husband, the writer, get a job?" She thinks, "Maybe I should get another one."

"I don't even think Nicholas likes having me home with him," I finally said. I could barely bring myself to admit this to her. "I think he's bored. When we walk in the park, all he wants to do is be with the other kids."

"Dave, he *loves* being with you."

"I think he wishes I had a job and he was in daycare. And to be honest with you, Pam, I like the sound of this job."

"Dave, you *have* a job," she said. "You're a writer."

"Let me apply, at least," I begged.

She said OK, but then a cloud passed over her face. She hugged Nicholas to her and said, "Oh, I don't know. He just seems so *young*."

I passed the first round of interviews with flying colours, talking a blue streak until they gave me the green light to see the silver-haired honcho.

That interview was over before it even began. After sitting in the reception area twiddling my thumbs for fifteen minutes, I walked into his huge corner office, which had exposed brick, floor-to-ceiling windows and framed posters of all the movies he'd made, and immediately knew I didn't have a hope in hell of landing the job. Why? Because there on his desk was a copy of *Chump Change*. Now, *Chump Change* may be, as one critic said, "brilliant and funny" (personally, I feel it is, although obviously, as the author, I find it hard to be objective), but it isn't exactly geared to endear me to prospective employers. The story concerns the spine-tingling misadventures of a certain "David Henry," an impoverished youngish writer who sells his soul to the devil for a job in TV news. He gets into one hair-raising scrape after another with producers, anchors and everyone else until—well, I don't want to give away the ending, but suffice it to say his TV career is as short-lived as it was ill-advised.

The silver-haired Shipwreck honcho told me he bought the book and read it over the weekend, said it even made him laugh out loud several times: "Something I rarely do when I read." He said his wife even had to ask him to pipe down.

"Thank you very much," I said. "I'm glad you enjoyed it."

Then, after a pause, he said, "Let me try to give you a sense of just what it is we do around here. We take people in their late twenties or early thirties and plug them into our formula—and make no mistake, it *is* a formula. If someone wants to be an auteur, this isn't the place for them. We have a certain way we do things, and it's been very successful for us."

I looked around his office and muttered something to the effect of "Yes, obviously. Congratulations."

"But you can learn the nuts and bolts of documentary filmmaking here, and after about four or five years a lot of the people who have worked here go on to make their own documentaries or do something else in the field."

This was the spot where normally I'd jump in and declare that what he'd just described, by some divine coincidence, was exactly the very thing I'd wanted to do my whole life, was my boyhood dream, in fact; and if you looked at my resumé in a certain light, what seemed to be a series of completely unrelated jobs with huge gaps between them were, in fact, stepping stones to the glorious career crescendo of Shipwreck Films. But something made me hold my tongue. I just couldn't land that whopper.

Which was for the best, actually, because the next thing out of his mouth was, "Now, you don't really want to be a documentary filmmaker, do you? You want to be a writer, and you've never wanted to be anything else. That's obvious from your book."

Busted. A relief, really. In a torrid rush, I blurted it all out: true, I'd always wanted to be a writer, but my wife had just had a kid and we needed cash, and I was staying home with him, going stir-crazy, and I became desperate, and I was really, really sorry to be wasting his time.

He was very nice about it all, considering. He told me not to give up, that I had genuine talent and I just needed to stay the course, and although he didn't know too much about these things, I'd probably wind up doing very well. But he also wrapped up our conversation quite quickly. After all, he was a busy man, and he still needed to find a *serious* candidate to fill his writer/producer position.

Well, that's it, I thought as I hit the sunshine and smog of the street. I now know that I am a househusband for the best and most traditional of reasons: I am not only unemployed but unemploy*able*. I was thirty-six, too old to bullshit someone into believing I wanted to start a whole new career in their profession. From here on in, it was househusband/writer or bust.

Anyway, I'm feeling better about myself and my role these days. I think the concepts of "stimulation" and "socialization" are overrated when you're talking about kids under four. I've read elsewhere that what kids need at that age is not so much stimulation and socialization but *guidance*, and they get that from having a full-time, dedicated adult around.

There are so many conflicting, confusing, contradictory studies, and they're all so politically and emotionally charged, it's hard to know the truth. In 1988, for example, a Pennsylvania State University psychologist named Jay Belsky did a study that suggested children who were in out-of-home care for more than twenty hours a week were more aggressive and clingy. Controversy rained down on Belsky's head, because even to hint that daycare might not be so great for kids is tantamount to suggesting women go back to being barefoot and pregnant in the kitchen. Finally, Belsky and his team of researchers were forced to "re-examine" the data and "modify" their findings. The results ran on page one of the New York *Times*: "Study Shows Daycare Not Harmful to Children."

I'm aware of the studies comparing home care favourably with daycare. I have one pinned to the wall of my office: "Lots of love good for child's brain, researchers say." The problem is these studies all talk about "maternal separation," and dads get only the odd joke mention. "The effects of maternal deprivation may be much more profound than we had imagined," the shrink in this study says, and causes brain cells in lab rats to die at an alarming rate. Even if Daddy Rat stays home? The study makes no reference to stay-at-home dads. We're still too tiny a statistical minority for researchers to bother with, I guess.

The only study I've seen that seems to apply to my situation is horribly outdated: a 1959 study called "Love in Infant Monkeys." A team of researchers at the University of Wisconsin separated rhesus monkeys from their mothers a few hours after birth and subjected them to a battery of tests. They found, among other things, that the little baby monkeys preferred a cloth-covered "mother substitute" over one made out of only chicken wire and wood (accompanying the text is a heart-rending picture of a baby rhesus clinging to his mother substitute, staring

searchingly into her bicycle-reflector eyes), even when the
chicken-wire "mother" was equipped with baby-bottle
"breasts." Which proved to those 1959 lab-coated geniuses
that an infant monkey's love for its mother isn't strictly a
survival reflex. Or to put it in their words, "our first experi-
ments have shown that contact comfort is a decisive vari-
able in this relationship."

They also found that when they put the baby monkey
and its cloth-covered mother in a strange room full of
strange objects, the infant monkey would explore, check
back with the cloth-covered mother, explore, check back
with the cloth-covered mother and so on. But if they
put the infant monkey in the same strange room with
the same strange objects with no mother or mother substitute, the monkeys crawled into a corner, threw themselves
face down, put their hands over their heads and screamed
in distress. "Records kept by two independent observers—
scoring for such 'fear indices' as crying, crouching, rocking
and thumb- and toe-sucking—showed that the emotional-
ity scores of the infants nearly tripled."

The study wraps up with an unabashed plea for more
monkeys to torture, in exchange for an endless vista of "sci-
entific" conclusions about the true nature of love: "The
further exploitation of the broad field of research that now
opens up depends merely upon the availability of infant
monkeys. We expect to extend our researches by undertak-
ing the study of the mother's (and even the father's!) love
for the infant, using real monkey infants or infant surro-
gates. Finally, with such techniques established, there appears to be no reason why we cannot at some future time
investigate the fundamental neurophysiological and biochemical variables underlying affection and love."

I love that exclamation point. . . . Yes, and using a cattle prod, blowtorch and pair of pliers, I'd like to investigate "the neurophysiological and biochemical variables" underlying the hubris of scientists who think they can tell us something new about love by torturing baby monkeys.

Anyway, I'm the cloth-covered "mother substitute." Lately, in an effort to assuage my guilt about Nicholas's "stimulation" and "socialization," I take him to a drop-in centre, where he can play with toys and other kids. It's a perfect compromise. As I write this, he's seventeen months old (which reminds me how slowly this book is coming along: "his milestones mock the funereal pace of our accomplishments," as I often say to people), still too young to interact in a meaningful way with the other kids, it turns out. He "parallel plays" alongside them; he is aware of them and sometimes interacts with them, but mostly he ignores them unless they try to take away something he's playing with or hit him over the head with a toy truck, both of which happen fairly often. What he mostly picks up from the other kids in the drop-in centre, it seems to me, are colds and bad manners.

I have noticed, though, that like an infant rhesus, Nicholas will explore, check with me, explore, check with me, and so on. I'm always there, and that has to count for something, right? Whenever he looks up, there's my big round face, watching over him like a pale patient moon. And if he falls, or one of the other kids pushes him, he looks around the room with big hot tears in his eyes. Where's Daddy? That looking-around-the-room-business, that's all I need to see to know I'm doing the right thing, despite everything.

8. THE POLITICS
OF DRUDGERY

In any case, since when do we turn to studies to tell us everything about how to live our lives? It's a curiously twentieth-century phenomenon to think a study can tell us how to raise children, conduct marriages and other relationships. One hundred and fifty years ago, if you wanted someone to believe in the truth of a statement, you would have begun it with "Poets say . . . " Now it's "According to a recent study . . . "

For me, it's a gut feeling. You bring a helpless little creature into the world, you take care of it, you hold it in your arms. I've since visited the daycare centre across the street. I looked around, got a pamphlet, even interviewed the director, shamelessly posing as a parent hoping to secure a place for his child. But what I was really seeking was self-justification, some sense that I was more than a super-annuated, hyperexpensive babysitter.

I found what I was looking for. The daycare staff were obviously a caring, qualified and nurturing crew, and, as advertised, there were numerous learning toys, not to mention a tunnel the kids could crawl through and the famous disco ball. But as I was touring the facility, I saw one of my friend's babies crying. The daycare worker was rocking her in her arms, comforting her, doing a good job of it, but staring off into the middle distance with a blank expression on her face; it was obvious she didn't love the child in her arms. "That's why I'm getting paid the big bucks," I said to myself. "For my love. I'm getting paid for my love."

I'm not criticizing people who put their kids in daycare. Everyone makes their own decisions, for their own reasons. Obviously, throughout human history, whenever anyone could afford to avoid the drudgery of caring for kids, they opted for it: governesses, wet nurses, boarding school, farming out, whatever. Out of twenty-one thousand babies born in Paris in 1780, for example, fewer than two thousand were kept at home. The other nineteen thousand were farmed out, usually deported to foster homes in the countryside, where many of them were fed a diet of wine-soaked bread and mashed chestnuts. And they survived—well, actually, they didn't. More than half of them died before the age of two from scurvy, dysentery and other diseases. But my point is: farming kids out is nothing new.

I'm aware that many people feel they can't afford to stay home with their children, although I would point out that in 1933, the average per capita income was less than half what it is today, and food, clothing and shelter accounted for almost 80 percent of the average family's income. When was the last time you wondered which cut of meat to buy, let alone whether you could afford meat at all? Anyone with a sense of domestic history, of how our grandparents lived versus how we live, knows the truth: we work harder because we spend more. In fact, we've *never been richer*.

Whereas I—I may not earn much, ladies, but I'm surprisingly cost-effective. I *husband* our family's resources. "Who *does* all this stuff in couples where both partners work?" I sometimes wonder as I push Nicholas around, picking up groceries, cleaning products, lamps and all the other little household details. The answer, of course, is a staff: nannies, sitters, waiters, delivery boys, fast-food chefs. Whereas once, as the proverbial African proverb says, it took a village to raise a child, now it takes a staff. One local newspaper recently hired an accountant to look through the books of a couple earning over $100,000, and although the wife's income was $33,000, after taxes and child-care expenses they only came out ahead by about $7,000.

Of course, $7,000 is $7,000 . . . but daycare's too institutional for my taste—too job-like. The babies report to the same impersonal fluorescent-lit building day in, day out; perform a set of routine activities from a roster pinned on the wall; spend their time crossing swords with people they may or may not like, as chance dictates; and in return are rewarded with . . . toys! "Ah, I get it now," I said to myself, looking around the daycare. "This is where it all begins. . . ."

Too recreational/consumerist a paradigm for me. I like it that when we're home and I wipe off the counter,

Nicholas will pick up a cloth and start trying to wipe off the walls. He sees that life is not only trading time for toys, there's work, too; in fact, work and play are inextricably intertwined. According to my private theory, very young children don't distinguish between work and play, they simply have projects. I don't want to discourage that. Viewed from a certain angle, you could say my whole life has been a struggle to harmonize work and play, to work for love and make my various projects pay off. Obviously, I'm still in the midst of that struggle. . . . Soon enough, I know, a giant juggernaut will be aiming its rays at Nicholas's tiny dome, trying to turn him into a consumer. He'll be going to school, and his peers will indoctrinate him into their Nintendo/Nike/Disney/Time Warner world view, and if I attempt to intervene they'll say, "Your dad's a crank, a freak. He's unhip, uncool, out of the loop. Here, strap this on, plug it into the wall socket, and you'll see what we mean."

But before they can get to him, fate has given me a few years to hang around with Nicholas, take him to the park, get ice cream cones, pat dogs, go to the grocery store, generally hang out together. A few years to become his friend and to earn his trust. These years won't come back, and Nicholas and I are building a relationship out of toy blocks and sofa cushions, using applesauce and yogourt as mortar.

The truth is, at this point, Nicholas would probably be fine in daycare. I'm the one who couldn't handle it, who would be filled with longing and "separation anxiety." Recently I've rejoined my local gym (after two years' absence, thinking, "I've *got* to lose the weight from Pam's pregnancy"). They have a babysitting centre where you can drop your kid off for a couple of hours while you work out.

The first time I went, Nicholas saw all the other kids and toys, and his attitude could be summed up as "Dad? Catch you later." He wouldn't even look up to say goodbye. I was going to work out for two hours, but I cut my workout short (though not, honesty compels me to admit, my post-workout steam bath), and went to pick him up after only an hour. Why? I missed him. I miss him when he's with Pam, when Audrey takes him out for a walk. Sometimes when he naps too long, I go in and wake him up. Why? I miss him.

And so my fate is fixed. . . .

But I don't want simply to stamp a big, round happy face on the whole business of househusbandry, for fear some poor, deluded slob out there will say to himself, "Hmmm, no office politics, hang around the house all day, bond with my kid, maybe change the odd diaper? I could handle that!" Then quit his job, stay home and slowly go out of his mind, staring at the four walls until they start to converge on him, winding up babbling and snickering to himself as he pushes his (empty?) pram down the street— ultimately blaming the whole sorry mess on me.

You see, I'm lucky. I live right across the street from a top-notch mental-health facility, so if I snap, it's just a hop, skip and jump into the arms of a team of trained professionals; whereas most people have to make a trip to the country, which seems like a bit of a bore.

I love looking after Nicholas. But as millennia of women know, it can be far from intellectually stimulating at times. "My heart is full but my mind is empty," is the phrase that keeps going through my head as I push him around. In her memoir, *Manhattan, When I Was Young,*

Mary Cantwell writes, "I had not spent all those days in classrooms and all those nights with John Donne so that I could spend my time washing Kate's little shirts and night-gowns and hanging them on the bathroom shower rail, separating B.'s shirts (they went to the cleaner at the corner) from the sheets and towels (they went to a big pick-up-and-deliver commercial laundry), and waiting for the diaper service man."

No. Nor when I was busting my hump getting not one but two master's degrees, one in English literature, one in journalism, did I ever imagine that I would be spending my days not only reading but memorizing stories with dialogue that goes "'Neigh, neigh,' said the horse. 'Want to go for a ride?'" or "'No, I'm Rhoda,' said a bear with a soda." Or narrative that goes "Monkeys drum, and monkeys hum. Hum drum, hum drum, hum drum hum."

"What's become of me?" I sometimes ask myself, as I push Nicholas along during the day, wondering what I should make for dinner that night, while my friends are at their offices, making money, going to lunch with clients and/or their assistants, hiring and firing. "Whatever became of David Eddie?"

It's ironic, really. I remember when I was fourteen or fifteen, looking at my father and thinking, "Where are your *friends*?" I thought his life was dull and boring, all about errands and paperwork. His dinner conversation was commensurately dull, dwelling as it did on the house, the mortgage, the car, the insurance, his dry dreary job as an economist ("the dismal science")—all matters I, the teenaged David Eddie, considered to be the "minutiae" of life. Once, I snuck a peek at his diary; all it talked about was what he had for breakfast, lunch and dinner.

"My life's never going to be that dull and boring!" I vowed. "All about errands and what I had for lunch! I'm going to meet interesting people, have outrageous adventures and erotic encounters in exotic locales! And I'm never going to do an errand in my life!"

I smile ruefully to myself, thinking back on that now, now that my entire life is lived within a three-mile radius. I *live* for errands; an errand is often the highlight of my day.

I deliberately stretch out errands to kill time. Say I need to get some broccoli (and I can feel my pulse quicken just thinking about it). I decide only the finest freshest broccoli, with the tightest purple-tipped florets, will do. I pop Nicholas in the stroller, visit every store in a three-mile radius, bend the ears of numerous shopkeepers en route, stop to pat every dog and chat with its owner, "What breed is it? Hmmmm . . . is that a good breed? Yes, I've been thinking of getting one for my boy, Nicholas, here."

All lies, I'm afraid. I don't really care for dogs: slobbering, sycophantic brutes, they get on my nerves; and I find the sight of them squatting in the park, their haunches trembling as they strain to push out a dark turd, frankly disturbing. But oh how I love human beings and long to hear their thoughts, no matter how trite, obvious and mundane. Dog owners tend to speak in whole sentences, each of which is like the strains of a Mozartian symphony to my homemaker's ears.

I kill time. I'm a minute murderer, an hour assassin. Or, to put it another way, I'm a time tycoon! If time is money, as they say, I have an embarrassment of riches (and it is an algebraic truth that if time equals money, money minus time equals zero). In a world in which most people don't even seem to have time to think, I'm thinking,

"Maybe I should bake my own focaccia? That would kill some time." It takes talent and dedication to kill as much time as I do. Sometimes I even find myself feeling proud of being one of the last practitioners of a dying art, like a Haida canoe-maker.

Other times, though, it doesn't feel so hot. "Househusband, eh?" a hearty handsome stockbroker said to me at a party the other day. "I'd do that—for a year." I was flabbergasted by the multi-tiered nature of this insult (tier 1: anyone could do it; tier 2: he'd only do it for a year—obviously, unlike me, the world couldn't spare him for longer than that; tier 3: his use of the conditional tense; in other words, he *could* do it, he *would* do it, but it's all hypothetical anyway, since obviously the world couldn't spare him for even a year). I mean, I know he meant well, but I wish I'd said, "No, you couldn't, pal. You'd be on the phone within six weeks, begging your boss to take you back. You couldn't handle the boredom, isolation, drudgery and lack of tangible rewards."

Actually, I guess that's a pretty depressing riposte, and I'm glad I kept my mouth shut. I get a lot of this kind of thing, though. There seems to be a mini-fashion among men these days to *claim* that they'd love to stay at home with their kids. In a 1997 Roper poll, for example, a quarter of men said they wish they could stay home with their kids. I wonder how many men could stand the actual day-to-day reality of it. To say it's simply boring would be an oversimplification. Looking after Nicholas has turned out to be a cornucopia of contradictions. It's everything at once, everything and its opposite: boring, yet fun; frustrating, yet rewarding; utterly banal, yet you feel what you're doing is important (like most jobs, I guess).

On the other hand, it is also true simply to say it's boring. I'm so tired of doing *dishes*. Even with a dishwasher, the dishes are eternal, immortal. And there are days when I feel so fed up dealing with the demands of a toddler, which are petty, irrational and constant. But I don't care. As I've said, I'll do anything to avoid having a job, even if it means working really, really hard. . . .

I am a drudge. I recall the day, the very hour, when this incontrovertible truth first presented itself to my consciousness. It was a Saturday morning, I was sitting in the kitchen reading the paper—Pam and Nicholas were at the park—and simmering up some stock from the chicken I'd roasted for dinner the night before. I make a lot of stock. It's easy (see Chapter 9, "How to Cook"). There's nothing better for you—why do you think they give it to you when you're sick? It freezes well, and it's indispensable for making soups, risotto and sauces. The French call stock *fond de cuisine*, the foundation of cooking. Stock is sort of like MSG, in that it makes everything you cook with it taste better. Making stock is never a mistake!

Except on this one particular occasion. I was reading an article about *Wallpaper* magazine and its founder, twenty-nine-year-old wunderkind (and local Toronto boy) Tyler Brûlé. An interesting story, actually: Brûlé had been a young reporter on assignment in Afghanistan when his car was caught in sniper fire. The driver was shot in the face. Armour-piercing bullets shattered Brûlé's right hand and severed nerves in his left arm (now he has a Bob Dole arm), but by some miracle everyone in the car survived.

Is it just me, or in the old days when people had near-death experiences didn't they vow to become more spiritual and less materialistic? Not Brûlé. Lying in hospital, recuperating from his injuries, he plumbed the depths of his soul and decided what he wanted in the time left to him was to be surrounded by beautiful things. Moreover, he wanted to found a magazine devoted to the celebration of beautiful things, called *Wallpaper* because it would be about "the stuff that surrounds you."™

Wallpaper started small, but since it was aimed at a potentially cash-flush target market—the Gen-X jet set, if you can imagine such a thing—deep-pocketed Time Warner snapped it up, *Wallpaper* went global, and Brûlé became golden. The article described Brûlé's fabulous lifestyle: the Concorde flights to New York; the starkly tasteful *Wallpaper* offices in London; *Wallpaper* story meetings, in which slim, black-clad twentysomethings stood around lobbing ironic, cross-referential comments into the air, all encased in invisible air-quotes as if to say, "I'm not 'really' 'saying' this"; Brûlé's ironic, cross-referential apartment, a subtle, multi-layered take on several generations of pop-culture kitsch and iconic tchotchkes; his beautiful suits and timeless timepiece (interesting to me was the fact that of all the "stuff that surrounded" Brûlé, the only thing that wasn't ironic and cross-referential was his wardrobe).

Yawn! I thought. Another generation takes up the reins of boring consumerism. If you pick up an anthology of younger Russian writers these days, you'll find they all talk about "the boring West." It's a given, a catchphrase. They take it for granted. "How could they say that?" you think at first. "With all our movies, television, music videos, etc." But that's precisely it: all that stuff has cretinized us. The West may be the most entertained culture in the history of humanity, but the least entertaining. Russians find our thoughts trite, obvious and simplistic: the typical reaction of a reading culture to non-reading savages.

Bored, I started to skip to the end of the article, but then came across a name that brought me up short. The reporter was canvassing various members of London's smart set, the fashion/magazine nexus, for their opinions on the upstart *Wallpaper*. And who should weigh in with her incredibly haughty and dismissive opinions? None other than The Princess herself! Remember her? My last girlfriend—last one I didn't marry, that is. Her career had obviously taken off since I'd seen her; she was described as the Fashion and Beauty Editor of either British *Vogue* or British *Cosmo*, I can't remember which.

"Oh, that's just great," I thought, sitting in the kitchen in my bathrobe, while my stock bubbled on the stove. "The Princess is part of London's smart set, and what am I? A frump, a drudge, sitting in a backward colonial capital, in my bathrobe, making chicken soup!"

That was the last thing I needed. Ever since I decided to become a writer, or acolyte of literature, I started training myself not to want too much in this life; to do without comforts most North Americans take for granted and live a disciplined, soldierly existence, if necessary; to endure whatever privations come my way with equanimity. Mostly it's been no problem. If I have one Achilles' heel, though, it's that I wouldn't mind being part of London's "smart set," rubbing elbows, clinking glasses and trading bons mots through bad teeth with various brilliant characters like Martin Amis. I don't know, Martin Amis would proba-bly avoid me like the plague, but this was my boyish dream.

And now The Princess had effortlessly parachuted into this milieu. To add insult to envy, I'd heard through the grapevine that the last time Her Royal Highness had deigned to visit our backward little burgh, our sparsely populated provincial capital, she'd been heard wondering aloud whether or not I, her ex, might not be "wasting his life" and "throwing away his talent."

Was I? Sure, I carry a notebook around everywhere I go, jotting down notes in coffee shops and restaurants, in doctors' offices and on top of newspaper boxes, even while sitting on the edge of the sandbox; I sit down in front of my computer for three to four hours every day; and I have my aggressive agent William in New York, who represents not only my literary properties but also those of Björk and Snoop Doggy Dogg. But maybe I'm kidding myself. Maybe househusband is what I really am, and writing is something I play at, I thought bitterly.

It was my first taste of what I've dubbed "housewife career envy," and it stung like a lash from an experienced and talented dominatrix. When Pam and Nicholas came home, Pam took one look at my face and said, "What's the matter?"

"Read this!" I said, shoving the newspaper at her.

"So?" she asked, when she'd finished.

"Recognize anyone's name in there?"

"Of course I do, Dave," she said. "What about it?"

"Oh, it just drives me crazy!" I expostulated, unable to contain myself any longer (while Nicholas stared up at me, wide-eyed, sucking on his pacifier). "What kind of world is this? World, where's your justice? Why her? Why not me? She's fashion and beauty editor, and what am I? A drudge, a frump, sitting in my bathrobe, making chicken soup!"

"Dave, take it easy," Pam said. "What are you getting so worked up about? You don't want to be a fashion and beauty editor. You never did."

"... true."

"So what are you freaking out about? Why are you jealous of her?"

"I'm jealous of everybody," I said, slumping down on the couch, staring at the rug and noticing how badly it needed vacuuming.

Pam was able to calm me down, as always, mostly by reminding me to count my blessings. And I do, I do. I don't want to become a "whinner," someone who whines while winning. (And I can hear those silent millennia of women saying, "He has one apparently well-behaved kid, various helpers and a dishwasher, and he complains about *drudgery*?") It's just that when you stay home with a kid, all everyone else in the world seems to be doing is pinning medals on each other and handing out awards and prizes, some with huge cheques attached. Meanwhile, everyone assumes that you, the faceless drudge, *le Cendrillon sans gueule*, have given up on all worldly ambition.

A couple of days later, my good friend Marcus came over with his twins. He's not a stay-at-home dad. Actually, his wife stays home full-time to look after the kids. But on Tuesdays he gets off work early and takes them off her hands so she can garden or read or pursue some other peaceful activity. It's no joke to look after twin toddlers by yourself: one tears off in one direction, bent on trouble; the other tears off in the other direction, also bent on trouble. What do you do? On Tuesdays he'd bring them to my place so they could fool around with Nicholas. The two of us would look after the three of them and meanwhile have a couple of cocktails, for God's sake.

"You know, I admire you for what you do, staying home

with Nicholas," he said on this occasion. "Not everyone could do it."

"Oh, it's no big deal," I said, misreading his meaning. "Anyone could do it. All it takes is patience and a little love."

"No, I mean—well, you know Amanda, right?"

I did indeed. In college days she was extremely beautiful, with a sexy wild streak that would come out sometimes late at night on the dance floor. Now she's a classic, one might even say *textbook* yuppie, a lawyer married to a lawyer. She drives around in a BMW with a cellphone glued to her ear.

"Yes," I said.

"Well, *she* could never do it. She put her kids in daycare after six weeks. You think they need the money? Believe me, they don't need the money. You should see their house. But she could never stay home with a kid." And then he said the fatal words "She's *too ambitious* for that."

That statement pushed all the wrong buttons, rang all the wrong bells.

"*What?*" I said. "What are you saying? That *I'm* not ambitious? Let me tell you something: I am the most ambitious person you know. I am the most ambitious person you'll ever meet. I'm *too ambitious* to be a lawyer. What do you think of that? I'm too ambitious to have a job!"

"OK, OK, take it easy, Dave. I know you're an ambitious guy. I . . . don't know what I was trying to say." He shrugged his shoulders and giggled.

Later, though, I thought, "Why did I have to be so emphatic?" Deep down, do I not consider bringing up Nicholas as important as writing?

Um . . . no. That's the long answer. No is the short answer. If it meant giving up my career, I'd have to put Nicholas in daycare. Who wants to give up their career? I don't. Pam doesn't want me to, either. She's even said so on national television, during a segment of a live chat show devoted to answering the question "Is there really such a thing as Mr. Mom?" I, the only actual specimen of *Homo domicilus* the producers could find, was naturally on the panel. Pam was sitting in the audience, and Nicholas was playing on the floor with another kid. The host paced back and forth with a microphone in his hand, intoning his intro. Then, in the manner of an investigative reporter, he thrust the microphone under my nose and asked me, "So. How do you like being called 'Mr. Mom'?"

"I would consider it an honour," I said, although (I told him) nobody's ever really called me that, and I don't consider myself very mom-like. My parenting style is very different, much more by the seat of the pants. But he was more interested in what Pam had to say. After all, they were colleagues, fellow broadcast professionals.

"What's it like to be married to a 'Mr. Mom'?" he asked her, thrusting the microphone under her nose.

"It's great," Pam said to my tremendous relief. She didn't want to give up her career, she told him, but she didn't want to put Nicholas in daycare, either; so this was a great solution. While she works, her kid's in good hands—or, at least, is being taken care of by someone who loves him.

"I *am* glad Dave has a career, though," she offered.

"What if he didn't?"

"I don't know. . . . I think that would be kind of weird," she said.

I made a mental note of this exchange, gentlemen, vowing never to let up on my career front, to remember it was the principal front of my life. Like a 1980s supermom, I want it all: my career plus the experience of staying home with Nick.

Here is a brief, admittedly outrageously oversimplified history of feminism. For thousands of years, women stayed home and did all the drudge-work. Then Betty Friedan wrote *The Feminine Mystique*, and women said to themselves, "Hey, wait a minute—this sucks!" They left their homes in droves to get jobs, money, power, respect, all the things men had been able to persuade them for so long they couldn't handle, didn't want, didn't need or flat out couldn't have.

But one matter never got sorted out: if everyone works, who looks after the kids? These days, it seems to me, couples who have children are presented with an almost insoluble dilemma. Even without a kid their lives were busy, and now they have this little unit (or units) needing twenty-four-hour care, feeding and attention. How do you swing it? Who wants to quit? Nannies are great if you can afford them, although you have to sort out the problem of your relationship to the nanny, and the nanny's relationship to your child. (It's worth it, perhaps: as Susan Cheever says in "The Nanny Track," "If there's a good woman behind every great man, behind every great *woman* there's a good nanny.") Daycare is an imperfect solution—public daycare was only ever intended as a temporary wartime measure so "Rosie the Riveter" could help our boys overseas.

Obviously I, as a househusband and stay-at-home dad, represent one extreme of the spectrum of solutions. Most people I know use a patchwork of nannies, grannies, mommy, daddy, babysitters, part-time and freelance work. Overall though, my observation from pushing Nicholas to the park and drop-in centre and all the rest of it is that the net result of the social revolution of the last thirty years is rich women now pay poor women to look after their kids and do the drudge-work. Children are still being looked after by women—just not their mothers.

Where are the men? Sometimes, while strollering along with Nicholas on a weekday, it seems to me that Gloria Steinem's dictum "a woman without a man is like a fish without a bicycle" is truer now than ever. Women can earn their own money, hire someone to look after their kids, *and* do most of the work around the house. What do they need men for?

To tell you the truth, I'm more worried about what all this drudgery and boredom is going to do to my personality than to my career. I'm haunted by an anecdote about Oscar Wilde, told by his good friend Robbie Ross, who was present at his death, about a lunch Wilde went to: "Oscar talked during lunch as I have never heard him talk before—divinely . . . Humour, tale, epigram, flowed from his lips and his listeners sat spellbound under the influence. Suddenly in the midst of one of his most entrancing stories—his audience with wide eyes and parted mouths, their food untasted—his wife broke in: 'Oh, Oscar, *did* you remember to call for Cyril's boots?'"

Oscar Wilde has always been, of all historical figures, my number one choice of dinner companion. Everyone who knew him says that his work was only a pale reflection of his conversation, which was unparalleled, hilarious, brilliant, "like the play of water in a fountain." Lately, though, I've found myself wondering if he *did* call for Cyril's boots. In other words, *I've started to sympathize with Oscar Wilde's dull, drab wife.* I'm starting to wonder if I would have enjoyed his talk, or would I have found it too purple, too lofty and impractical, not down-to-earth enough.

Perhaps, I've been thinking lately, Pat Mainardi was right in her devastating 1970s essay "The Politics of Housework" when she wrote, "In a sense all men everywhere are slightly schizoid—divorced from the reality of maintaining life. This makes it easier for them to play games with it. It is almost a cliché that women feel greater grief at sending a son off to war or losing him to that war because they bore him, suckled him, and raised him."

I definitely feel that changing diapers and all the rest of it has made me a more practical person than before. Men are starting to seem so clueless to me, on this front. By adopting the woman's traditional role, I've become more aware of the edifice of drudgery—the mountain of dishes, laundry and diapers—that stands behind every adult achievement. It's also true that, having been intimately involved in the care and feeding of Nicholas, I'm less likely to send him off to war with unmixed enthusiasm. I bust my hump for eighteen years to get a telegram from the army saying he died in some jungle or desert? I don't think so.

And drudgery can be quite inspiring. "The best time to plan a book is when you're doing the dishes," Agatha Christie said, and I agree. As I scrub, mop, clean, dust and cook, thoughts are always popping into my head; and I keep a typewriter on each floor of the house, with a piece of paper in the roller, so I can type them up before I forget them.

"Phew, you need to get out more, Dave," you may be saying. "Now it appears you're actually advocating boredom and drudgery." I'm not; all I'm saying is someone has to do it, and anyway, you're probably right. This is probably all a grandiose attempt at rationalization of my role, and I should just stick to the facts: 1) I stay home with Nicholas because I'm a loser; 2) it's boring.

I do miss having a certain measure of freedom. Right now, in order to go to the corner store, in winter anyway, I have to enter into a major battle with Nicholas, a battle to get him into his coat, hat, boots and mittens, while he squirms like a rhesus monkey, screams, slugs me in the nose, grabs my specs, yanks off his boot and chucks it across the room, and so on. It's tiring. What I miss is simply the freedom to say "sure" if someone invites me out for a cup of coffee.

But then, what would I do with that kind of freedom anyway? If I weren't doing this, would I not be engaged in a pursuit equally mind-numbing? At least I'm not a "marketing and promotion manager for a line of quickie biscuits," as I heard someone describe his occupation recently, or something equally absurd. At least looking after a kid feels worthwhile on some level. At least I don't have to pretend to like it, the final murder of the soul. I could never join the office hordes. Every time I try, I'm summarily ejected, like a circus clown from a cannon. Clearly, my destiny lies elsewhere.

And it's not true that life with Nick is entirely free of adventure. We go on adventures together. When he was about one and a half we went together to visit my grandmother Kate, my father's mother, who was dying of throat cancer, but also, at ninety-one, of old age, in Deer Lake,

Minnesota. "It's a choice between visiting her now or coming to the funeral," Dad told me. I opted to see her while she was still alive and to bring Nick along, so he could meet her.

As usual, I had pre-flight jitters. It hadn't been so long before this that Swissair Flight 111 dropped out of the sky off the coast of Peggy's Cove, Nova Scotia. Why did it happen? They're not sure. But they think the wires in the in-flight entertainment system might have shorted out.

"The entertainment system!" I shouted at my friend Patrick, who was over for a drink the day before I left. "All those people had to die—and they had something like eleven minutes during which they *knew* they were going to die, by the way, before plummeting into the Atlantic Ocean—for the sake of *in-flight movies*! I'd rather read a book!"

"Take it easy, Dave," he said. "It won't happen to you."

"That's what everyone on Swissair Flight 111 thought!"

He shrugged, and sipped his drink.

"What about Pam?" I said. "She'll be horribly bereaved if we get in a crash."

"She'll get over it. Just to be on the safe side, though," he said, laughing, "maybe you should leave a turkey baster full of sperm in the freezer."

"Thanks," I said. "That's really helpful."

The law requires that a gentleman travelling alone with a baby bring a note from the mother testifying that she knows about it, and the child is not being abducted. Pam and I were informed of this at the gate, just before the flight took off.

"What?" I asked the customs officer. "Do women travelling alone with babies have to carry a note from the father?"

The customs officer looked at me like I had asked the question in Urdu.

"I mean, why do only men need the note?" I asked.

He shrugged. "Is this your wife? Why don't you just get her to write you a note?"

It took two planes to get us there, one from Toronto to Minneapolis, then a little twenty-four-seater eggbeater plane from Minneapolis to Grand Falls. Nicholas behaved like a champ the whole time. I think he knew I needed him to be good, and he rose to the occasion. That night as I put him down in a strange crib in a strange house, he looked up at me as if to ask, "This is OK, right, Dad?" I suddenly re-alized that for all he knew, I was abandoning him here in this strange house, in a strange crib, for typically in-scrutable adult reasons, and he would never see me or his beloved mother again.

"It's all right, Nick," I whispered to him. "Everything's fine. I love you, and I'll see you in the morning. In the meantime, if you need me, I can be here in a flash."

"Flash," Nicholas repeated and rolled over to go to sleep, sucking on his pacifier.

I wouldn't want to miss moments like that. What is life, anyway, but a series of moments? What do we talk about at memorial services but moments we shared with the de-ceased? Nor would I want to miss moments like the next morning, when we went to the nursing home, and Nicholas put his tiny little hand on his great-grandmother's knobby-jointed, wizened old claw that lay mostly motionless on the bedspread—and patted it.

"Oh, that feels nice," she whispered hoarsely (the can-cer was attacking her throat), eyes closed, heavily sedated with morphine.

"He's cute, isn't he, Grandma?"

"I'll say," she said, on that, the last occasion I saw her. Nick was a champ on the way back, too. I'm glad I brought him (we didn't go to the funeral). He met his great-grand-mother. I think he remembers her too. A little while ago, at the museum, he went up to a painting of an old lady and said, clear as a bell, "Kate!"

Even when we stay in the city, we have adventures—just on a much lower level, and also lower to the ground. The radius, circumference and scope of my adventures have shrunk, but there's more attention to detail. The depth of field has narrowed, but objects are brought into sharper focus. We can have a dozen mini-adventures on the way to the corner store: a fire truck might go by; he might spot a bug; someone might be out walking their dog, which is always the highlight of his day. "Doggie!" Then, to the owner, "Pat it?"

As I introduce Nicholas to my world—a world of coffee shops, bookstores, bars, grocery stores and bank machines—he's introducing me to *his*: a world of dogs, soap bubbles, candy, sandcastles, toy trains, imaginary bears, cookies, planes, dump trucks and Popsicles. It's a beautiful world, and hanging around Nicholas has been good for my (bitter, cynical, skeptical) personality, I think. I often tell people, if they feel upset, stressed out or sick of it all, "You know, you should spend less time with other people and more time with Nicholas." I *prescribe* this to them, like a doctor prescribes an Aspirin. It's definitely worked for me. I'm a better person than I was a year ago. I can feel it.

9. HOW TO COOK

"As a youth, I used to weep in butcher's shops."
   – Monty Withnail, *Withnail and I*

"So, your wife brings home the bacon, and you cook it up, eh?" a lot of people ask me these days, usually followed by a hearty har-har and a slap on the back.

Actually, I prefer it if she brings home the pancetta. As my culinary mentor, Marcella Hazan, puts it, bacon's "smoky accents tend to weary the palate." But, yes, that's the general idea. She makes the money. I'm the cook.

I love to cook. That statement alone would amaze anyone who knew me, say, ten years ago and had somehow fallen out of touch. If you met someone of that description and told her, "Dave's a cook now. He's the main chef of his family," she'd say, "Dave Eddie? Are you sure we're talking about the same guy?"

In my twenties, I think I tried to cook *once*. Max and I were at my mother's place for some reason. She was away, we were stoned and had the munchies, and we tried to make a tuna casserole in her kitchen. It *should* have worked. We put in some cheese, some noodles, some mayo I think, olives and I don't remember what all else. But the result, when it came out, was so nasty, noxious and noisome, we literally had to *run* out of the kitchen to get away from it. We didn't have to taste it. All we had to do was get a whiff of it.

"Argh, what a terrible odour," Max said as he pulled it out of the oven.

"It smells *foul*," I concurred.

"Let's get out of here."

"Yeah," I said. "Let's *run*."

(Reflecting back on that heinous casserole, Max now theorizes that one ingredient, some paprika paste my father had brought back from Hungary many years before, had a sort of domino effect on the other ingredients; or, as he puts it, "caused the casserole to seize up like a car engine running without oil.")

But poverty is a great teacher, they say; it certainly taught me how to cook. During my Bachelor Hell phase, working only two days a week, trying to write, I was also living in the midst of an open-air market: Kensington Market, "the breadbasket of Toronto." I was surrounded by a cornucopia of fruits and vegetables, not to mention butchers' shops with whole goats, half pigs and every possible part of a cow—hooves, lungs, tongues, even eyeballs—attractively displayed in the windows. Also bakeries, cheese shops and stores featuring dried foods of every description: rice, pasta, coffee grounds, dried fruits, nuts and spices. Meanwhile, I pursued a typical bachelor diet: pizza slices, burgers, take-out Chinese, processed cheese slices sandwiched between two bagel-halves and wrapped in plastic film. *Maybe* the odd apple or banana when I was thinking of going on a health kick. And of course I washed it all down with a steady stream of alcoholic beverages, coffee and diet cola; then fired up a cigarette. I hardly tasted my food, thinking of it as fuel, gobbling it all down while talking to someone or reading a book.

But there came a time when I said to myself, "Hmmmm . . . I'm surrounded by all these raw fruits, vegetables and meats. I wonder if there's some way all these raw materials could actually be transformed into something I could eat."

So I began to cook, slowly at first, then with increasing confidence. I acquired several recipe books, including one my mother gave me, which was written for the mentally challenged: *The Trinity Square and Cawthra Square Cafe Cookbook.* The basic principle behind cooking, it turns out, is simple: you put what you want to eat near something hot for a while, then eat it. With some foods—like sushi, carpaccio and antipasti—you don't even have to do that. All you have to do is take what you want to eat and *put it out.* What's generally called cooking should really be called food processing: you process the food to the point where you can eat it. What everybody has to decide is where they want to place themselves on the spectrum. Do you want to buy a freshly killed chicken, maybe with its feet still on, or a hermetically sealed box of frozen, microwaveable chicken chunks?

"The chunks, the chunks!" you may say. "Give us the chunks! We'll take the chunks *every time.*" And that's fine. But in an era in which so much of our food is genetically engineered and produced by biotech companies, I like to get as close to the farmer as I can. For the most part, I prefer the creations of God over the creations of mankind. I know it's impossible to prove at the moment why genetically altered foods, which compose a huge proportion of U.S. crops (genetically engineered Roundup Ready seeds by Monsanto, for example, account for 30 percent of U.S. soybeans and 15 percent of corn—which is a lot of soybeans and corn), are bad for you, but I'm sure one day we'll find out that they are. I can just see the media conference, the lab-coated geniuses saying, "What we didn't realize when we were working on this project..." No thanks!

In my twenties, if I took you on a tour of my apartment, and we came to the bedroom, I'd lower my voice and say in a histrionic whisper, "This . . . is where it all happens." Now, though, I'd have to say that about the kitchen. The kitchen has taught me a basic truth: whatever else you are—cabinet minister, busboy, porn star, pilot—you are also an organism. I'm amazed by how many of my friends live their lives as if each meal were the last they'll ever need. It's like "Ah, I'm full. Guess I'll never have to eat again." Then a few hours later, they'll say, "Hey, there's that strange, rumbling feeling in my stomach again."

I love asking my bachelor friends the following question: "What do you *usually* eat for dinner?"

"What do you mean, *usually*?" they'll reply, suspiciously. "There *is* no usually." Or they might say, as my friend Max once did, "It's usually some combination of having a sandwich and eating out." In other words, he might have a sandwich, or he might go out, or he might go out and have a sandwich, but he would almost never do neither. I will note in passing that the Italian "Cubano" sandwich—roast pork, aïoli, avocado and onion—seems to be the sandwich of choice among my bachelor brothers.

Whereas I now look at the whole world through a food-based lens. I can't even watch a rock video these days without thinking, "I wonder what those kids are eating." I wouldn't describe myself as a foodie. I think you can put too much importance on food, like anything else— drugs, booze, sex, yoga, TV—if you wrap your whole life around it, you risk becoming a bore. However, I think the tendency here in North America is to think about food too little. As Margaret Visser, the great historian of the everyday, says in *Much Depends on Dinner*, "We echo the preferences and the principles of our culture in the way we treat our food. An elaborate frozen dessert moulded into the shape of a ruined classical temple can be read as one vivid expression of a society's view of itself and its ideals; so can a round ground hamburger patty between two circular buns."

I've spoken elsewhere about the importance of cooking to a bachelor, which I believe to be more or less self-evident: it's cheaper, so you can spend more on the wine; it's more intimate, since you choose the mood and music; you demonstrate your competence and ability to take charge of a situation; above all, at the end of the meal, *you're already in your apartment*. No will-she, won't-she at the threshold. But what a lot of people fail to grasp is the supreme importance of cooking to the married or cohabiting man. Especially when you have a kid. Just after birth: that's when the true uselessness of modern man becomes glaringly apparent, in my opinion. She's lying there, recovering, and he can't even keep her fed. A change occurs in their relationship. She gets the "moral high ground" and never loses it thenceforward. The man is established as a bumbling fool, superfluous, absurd and possibly even malefic, and he tends to remain on that footing.

Learning to cook can change all that. You can never truly be in the doghouse if you're turning out little snacks and treats. Just as you build your own doghouse, it is also true that you make your own brownie points. Besides, there's no better antidote to spending a day in front of a keyboard. "To the victor go the spoils," they say, but who wants the spoils? To the cook go all the tasty little tidbits. So here's a little guide for the culinarily challenged, beginning with a couple of introductory observations.

Pick a cuisine and stick to it, at least at first, so you can evolve a pantry full of spices and stock items that you use all the time. For me, it's Italian, the mother of all cuisines. (Even *Larousse Gastronomique*, the bible of the French kitchen, admits modern French cuisine began when Catherine de' Medici brought her entourage of cooks from Florence to France for her marriage to the future King Henry II). I like Italian because it's straightforward, unpretentious and *subtle*. The taste buds tend to tire of the stronger flavours in some other cuisines. If you think of food as basically an accompaniment to wine, as I do, I think you're forced to agree that either Italian or French cuisine is the best accompaniment to a delicious bottle of, say, Amarone. Most of all, I like classic Italian because it is at heart a housewife's cuisine; unlike classical French cookery, which seems more geared towards restaurants. In classic Italian cooking there are only about thirty basic ingredients you need in your cupboard or fridge, including

Parmigiano-Reggiano, sea salt, pancetta, prosciutto, canned tomatoes, dried porcini mushrooms, pasta, "oo" flour, garlic, anchovies, nutmeg, capers, red pepper flakes, olives, olive oil, balsamic vinegar, bread crumbs, a few dried herbs (oregano, thyme, sage, rosemary) and fresh flat-leaf parsley and basil. With these items you lie in wait for whatever is fresh and in season.

Better yet, pick a single mentor. My mentor is the earthy-yet-divine Marcella Hazan, author of *Marcella Cucina* and *Essentials of Classic Italian Cooking*, among other indispensable classics (I count *Essentials of Classic Italian Cooking* among the books that changed my life, like *The Little Prince, Steppenwolf, Money* and *Notes of a Dirty Old Man*). Marcella Hazan is a big part of the reason we in North America even know what extra-virgin olive oil is, or balsamic vinegar, or Parmigiano-Reggiano. Part of the reason I love her is because she's so draconian: she brooks neither fools nor substitutions. You can cheat on her recipes, take a shortcut, substitute pre-grated Parmesan for Parmigiano-Reggiano, say ("if you enjoy the taste of sawdust"). Of course you can. What's it got to do with her? She washes her hands of you. She cannot understand people who cook without passion, dedication, and love—who, in short, aim no higher than mediocrity.

I also love her because, like me, she started cooking for strictly homely reasons, albeit with a particularly exacting spouse, the food and wine critic Victor Hazan. She has a housewife's practicality, though she also tends to assume you have quite a bit of time on your hands. I do. After Nicholas goes to bed, I cook, and we eat late—what else are we going to do?

Besides time, here are a few other things you'll need:

Love

People can actually *taste* the love and care you put into the preparation of food, in my opinion. Take coffee. The exact same ingredients go into the worst diner dishwater swill as into the most delicious cappuccino: water, coffee and sugar. The cappuccino tastes better because the ingredients are handled with love, respect and care. By the same token, a lot of people feel sandwiches taste different depending on how you cut them, and I agree. (They taste better cut on the bias.)

Humility

Humility and respect for the millennia of cooks who have gone before you. Sometimes I'll experiment, and it won't work out, and I'll think, "Some Roman housewife probably made this same mistake two thousand years ago." Made it, and then passed her knowledge to her daughter, who passed it to her daughter, and so it went down through the generations, getting amplified, modified, revised, tinkered with, added to and subtracted from. You can't possibly hope to learn all that in a single lifetime. That doesn't mean you shouldn't experiment; trying things out and failing is part of the process. Remember that "in every cook's life, the occasional soufflé will fall." But before you can experiment successfully, you have to know the form, just as before you can write decent free verse, you have to master the sonnet form.

Good Ingredients

Cooking begins at the market; I'm amazed more cook-books don't stress this (the word *recipe* comes from the Latin "to procure"). With ultra-fresh ingredients, you can cook just about anything briefly and drizzle it with a bit of olive oil and sea salt (or the greatest of salts, *sel gris*, if you can find it), and it will be hailed as "gourmet." Ideally, you have to have a relationship not only with your butcher, but also with your fishmonger and greengrocer, so they can tell you, as my greengrocer did the other day, "Why don't you try those apples? They're the first of the fall." The apples he recommended were amazing, crisp and juicy, like biting into the essence of fall.

You also have to be flexible. As the divine Marcella ob-served in a cooking class I had the privilege to attend, "I might be planning to cook meat on a given night, but if I go to the market and have the good fortune to spot a fish twitching on the ice, I change my plans."

Knowledge of Basic Formulae

There are a couple of basic formulae to making dinner. Probably the most basic is the old British formula: meat plus two veg equals dinner, although technically one of the two veg isn't a veg at all, but a carbo, like rice or potatoes. I can't count how many dinners I've made based on this for-mula. I pick up a couple of pork chops at the market and think, "Hmmm, we have some spinach in the freezer. Do we have any potatoes?" With seasonings, it's a perfectly acceptable family meal.

The second formula is salt plus fat equals flavour. All

fast-food outlets know this. So do most other restaurants. Only at the loftiest pinnacles of the art of cookery are those who have learned to balance sweet with acid and other insider's tricks. But those of us toiling in the trenches know that a pinch of salt and a pat of butter or drop of oil, judiciously applied, can work wonders.

And for God's sake don't forget:

Presentation

So important. "The first taste is with the eyes," as they say. Restaurants know this too. The food at most restaurants is usually nothing so special or difficult—they have to churn out too many meals to give them their best—but it's so well presented you don't even notice. I can hardly eat in a restaurant these days; I wind up feeling too ripped off. I only go for ideas.

Remember: your guests *want* to believe, they *want* to think you've become this great chef. As Bob Fosse put it in the musical *Chicago*, "Razzle-dazzle them, and they'll make you a STAR!"

The Satori of Cooking

I have found over the course of being the family's "primary provender preparer" that there's a certain satori of cooking, that the stock from last night's roast chicken becomes today's soup and tomorrow's risotto, etc. So rather than offer a series of discrete recipes, I thought what I might do is take several recipes that sort of flow into each other. And these recipes, like my cooking style, don't concern themselves too much with measurements and exact amounts—

like Toulouse-Lautrec's cookbook, *The Art of Cuisine*, in which recipes might start with "take a whole sheep" or tell you to "throw in a handful of lard" or whatever.

In short, don't sweat the details, gentlemen. Cooking is just like barbecuing, only it happens indoors.

How to Roast Meat and Potatoes

I'm amazed that the housewives of the 1950s could get away with portraying roasting as something difficult and exhausting. Roasting is the easiest thing in the world to do. Here's the recipe for roast chicken: grab the chicken firmly by the legs and wings, put it in a pan and slide it into the oven. That's about it. Of course, it helps if the oven's actually on, at about 350 degrees, and you should thoroughly wash everything before you cook it, including the chicken, inside and out, and pat with paper towels. You can rub it with salt, too, and garlic and rosemary. It's done when you cut into it all the way to the bone and the meat's all white and the juices run clear. Slice it up and slap it on the plate.

You can use the same method to cook any meat. Same for spuds. The single dish I serve this little family most often is roast potatoes. Here is the ridiculously easy yet delicious and practical recipe we stole from Pam's sister, Alison: Peel two spuds, cut into chunks; peel onion, cut into chunks; peel entire head of garlic and separate into individual cloves; throw into loaf pan, drizzle with olive oil and sprinkle with salt; bake one hour, stirring occasionally. Crispilicious every time.

How to Boil Vegetables

Take just about any vegetable, peel and/or cut it up, rinse thoroughly and throw it into a large pot of boiling salted water. When it's tender yet crisp, it's done. The only drawback to this method for preparing vegetables is the nutrients leach out into the water. Like my mother before me, I actually drink the greenish, brackish water for extra nutrition. But that's me. . . . Another, quicker method to do veggies is to stir-fry them in a little olive or other oil, maybe with a whole peeled clove of garlic for flavour. Somehow, though, I don't think this tastes as fresh and light as the boiling method. PS Don't throw away the stems of broccoli; peel and chop those up too. Marcella Hazan's husband, Victor, won't even eat the florets. He considers them "an accident of nature" and won't touch them. I don't go that far; however, I do think the stem is the best part, and it's a tragedy if you throw it away.

How to Keep Your Cool

One semi-tricky bit about cooking is timing everything to reach fruition at exactly the same moment. This used to cause me—and our relationship—a great deal of stress. Before dinner parties, especially, I, stressed out, would invariably snap at Pam, call her contributions to the dinner "pointless" and "irrelevant." She would respond indignantly, and we'd have a horrible argument. When our guests arrived, we'd be emotionally drained, pale and shaky. Everyone knew about these tiffs, to the point where Patrick, entering the kitchen, handing over a bottle of wine, kiss-kiss, would say, "Had your pre-dinner argument yet?"

One way to avoid these preprandial contretemps is to serve your dinner in classic Italian style, which is to serve numerous small courses, such as soup, then rice, say, then meat or fish, then *insalata*—but then you never get to talk to your guests. On the one occasion I was lucky enough to meet and actually have a smoke with the divine (yet earthy) Marcella—outside, during a break in a class she gave at The Bonnie Stern School of Cooking—I asked her, "When you're having a dinner party, how do you serve a meal in the Italian style and still interact with your guests?"

I hastily explained I was the cook in the family. She took a drag of her cigarette and considered. Other eager acolytes were milling about, itching to ask her *their* pesky questions, but I planted myself with feet apart right in front of her (albeit down a couple of steps), interposing my enormous bulk between them and my goddess of food.

"When you have people over," she said finally, in sage tones tinged with her heavy Italian accent, "what does your wife do? Does she cook?"

"Well, she helps a bit, but mostly she cleans up the house and then, when people come over, serves drinks and takes their coats."

"Then it is simple," she decreed. "Listen. When people come to your house for dinner, they want you to cook them a meal. So, cook."

But I don't know. With all due respect to Marcella, I flatter myself that I have more to offer my guests than the sight of my tightly clenched, stressed-out derrière in front of the stove. I agree with Sally Quinn, the *Washington Post* columnist, who says in her book *The Party* that when you have people over, it's not so much about the food, it's about the conviviality and the drinks, and you should make something easy (though she takes this notion a bit far with her bacon-mushroom–ground beef casserole and other dreadful-sounding dishes).

It's a ticklish problem. One solution is to roast everything. Cooking times are approximate, and everything can stay warm in the oven. In general, the more things you roast, the less stress you, as the host, will have.

Or, if it's a warm summer night, you can actually serve a *cool dinner*. Credit for this idea goes to my friend Linda. She served a "cool dinner" one muggy evening at her fabulous mansion: cool salmon, cool potatoes and cool asparagus. It was a revelation. Instead of Linda slaving away in the kitchen and feeling exhausted while serving the meal, we sat around, elegantly attired, sipping cocktails on her picturesque porch, and then had dinner at our leisure, at what appeared to be a propitious moment.

You can serve a cool dinner with almost anything. If, for example, in the above meat-plus-two-veg-meal, your veg was green beans, you could cook the whole thing two hours in advance, drizzle the beans with olive oil and sprinkle with salt, leave everything in little bowls and serve later. The spuds might suffer a bit, but my point is there's no real rush. This technique works well with a variety of foods, and if you do serve your food cool, may I suggest you throw in

A Little Fresh Salsa?

Always impresses. My favourite of all time is Linda's from that magic cool-dinner night. Simply cut a mango into little chunks, add some chopped red onion, a couple of chopped jalapeño peppers, juice squeezed from a couple of fresh limes (don't even *think* of cheating on this ingredient, and remember the other rule of cooking: the fewer the ingredients, the higher the quality each one has to be) and some chopped, *washed* coriander. That's it. Mix and serve. Your guests will freak out, and only you, the clever little chef, need know how easy it all is.

How to Make Stock

But to get back to the satori of cooking. After your roast chicken dinner, what I think is sort of fun, in a medieval way, is to throw the carcass, bones, skin and meat into a huge stock pot, add some whole celery stalks, a whole carrot, *exactly* six peppercorns—one more or one less will ruin the whole thing! (just kidding)—a bay leaf or two and an onion, whole or chopped in quarters, and simmer on low heat for two hours, partially covered. Then strain through a colander into another pot, discarding the solids, and put the liquid in the fridge. Overnight, the chicken fat will rise to the top and congeal. This you scrape off, obviously, and the liquid that remains is called stock. For best results, strain it through a colander lined with cheesecloth (paper towels don't really work). Then you can freeze it in jars, or (best method, but a bit time-consuming) freeze it in ice trays, take out the cubes and plop them into zip-lock freezer bags. Then you can use as much as you want, taking out a cube or a fistful of them at a time. I always keep some frozen to add here and there to a stir-fry or whatever. But stock keeps for three or four days in the fridge, so here are two excellent ways to use it up before it expires. You can throw just about anything in it and call it soup, or else you can learn:

How to Make Risotto

"Rice is holy food," I'll often pontificate to Pam, "the main source of sustenance for more than half the people on the planet. Much of human history and civilization is the direct result of man's efforts to cultivate and harvest rice, and if we ate a more rice-based diet, probably half our problems would be solved." To which she indignantly responds that the potato is equally holy and has also played an important role in history.

Either way, I make a lot of risotto. To me, risotto is the most comforting of comfort foods, a stew of rice that nonetheless has an al dente crunch, and I can't get enough of it. You have to do it right, though, stand there stirring it like a slave for half an hour (something restaurants almost never do, and I'm shocked at what I've been served under the heading "risotto"), and then, according to the divine Marcella, you must serve it within ninety seconds of it being finished or "it's not risotto. It's flavoured rice, which is also delicious, but it's not risotto."

"Who needs it?" you might say. "Too much work." But that's what I like about it. Making risotto is for me what playing golf is for other men: so stressful and absorbing I forget all my other worries while I'm doing it. And anyway, it's actually quite quick. I have a whole risotto-making ritual, like a Japanese tea ritual: two measuring cups, one with two cups of rice, either arborio, vialone nano or carnaroli, and one with five cups of homemade stock; two pots, a large, heavy-bottomed one on the left front burner for the risotto, and a smaller one on the right front burner for the stock; a small bowl to the right of the right burner, in which rests a soup ladle; to the left, the various ingredients.

Risotto can be made with almost anything—sausage, green beans, yellow peppers, prosciutto, zucchini, asparagus, porcini mushrooms—whatever you think would taste good with the subtle backdrop of white rice, butter and Parmigiano-Reggiano.

Sauté a chopped onion in butter over a medium-low flame until golden—it could take ten minutes or more. Most people tend to under-sauté onions, which weakens their "flavour base" (in Italian cooking, sautéeing the onions and/or garlic is called *insaporire*, meaning "to bestow flavour"). Meanwhile, bring the stock to a simmer. Pour the rice into the pan with the onions, stir for one minute, fry it a bit, then stir in a ladleful of stock. Keep stirring. With risotto you have to stir pretty much non-stop. Good risotto rice is characterized by a hard kernel surrounded by a soft starch called amylopectin. The idea is to break down the amylopectin into a starchy soup while the internal kernel is still al dente. So it makes no matter if it gets a little dry. The kernels rubbing together and against the hot pot are what breaks down the amylopectin. So keep adding ladlefuls of stock, and keep stirring. The risotto is done when it's soupy yet al dente. Then quickly stir in a little more butter and some Parmigiano-Reggiano. Spoon onto heated plates, then spastically sprinkle more Parmigiano-Reggiano everywhere and, if you wish, a tiny bit of flat-leaf parsley all over the rice, the plate, the counter (corny presentation cliché, but it works). *Mangia!*

OK, enough satori of cooking. You've just served two family dinners in a row. Congratulations! On night three, order pizza, or "box of groceries," as my bachelor friends call it. The next night, take it easy and make:

Pasta Dave Eddie

Like its creator, the pasta that bears my name is piquant, elegant yet earthy, and almost impossible to fuck up. I've seen people who try to rip this recipe off me forget to put in the Parmigiano-Reggiano or the lemon or substitute shrimp for chicken. It's still delicious, the talk of the town. Bring a huge pot of salted water to a boil. In another pan, sauté onions in olive oil until they're golden, and one chopped chicken breast until it's white. Splash in a little white wine, simmer until the alcohol has evaporated (you can smell it leaving the pan), about one minute. Squeeze in the juice of one lemon, and add exactly nineteen pitted olives, twenty pickled capers (without any juice, use a fork to get them out of the bottle), salt and pepper. Stir a bit, add some grated Parmigiano-Reggiano (among its many other excellent qualities, true Parmigiano-Reggiano thickens sauces without becoming stringy), and turn off the heat. The pasta sauce can sit there a while, no problem. Later, you'll heat it up by tossing it with the hot pasta. Drop pasta, ideally penne, into boiling salted water, and cook eight to ten minutes or until *molto al dente* (extra chewy). Drain, then toss the pasta in a large heated bowl with the sauce. Serve on plates or in shallow pasta bowls, after having sprinkled fresh ground pepper and more cheese all over the bowl like a lunatic. Guaranteed 100 percent delicious. Afterwards you can serve

Warm Escarole Salad

This recipe was actually inspired by a kid's story, *The Very Hungry Caterpillar*. The very hungry caterpillar eats, on one day, a piece of chocolate cake, a pickle, a slice of Swiss cheese, a slice of salami, a lollipop, a piece of cherry pie, a sausage, a cupcake and a slice of watermelon. After that, as you can imagine, he had a stomach ache. But then he eats through a leaf and feels better.

"Yes!" I said to myself after reading this book to Nicholas a couple of thousand times. "We should end all meals by munching through leafy greens."

But I've always found salads boring, too crunchy and fresh. Now I'll often end meals with this half-cooked course. Simply brown a clove of garlic in a wok or large pan. This lends an accent of garlic to the oil, without the overpowering presence of actual bits of garlic. Then toss in washed, torn-up escarole or other leafy greens and salt, and cook, tossing frequently, until it's not quite wilted (this takes a bit of practice) and serve in individual bowls.

And . . . um, that's about it for my repertoire. Other than these items, I make stir-fries out of pretty much whatever we have in the fridge and make it up as I go along. The main thing to remember here is the stir-fry is basically a condiment, and what you're eating is a bowl of rice. As Confucius says, you shouldn't eat so much meat that your breath "smells of meat rather than of rice." The word for rice in Chinese, *fan*, also means food. The word for everything else, *ts'ai*, basically means relish, something you sprinkle on the rice to make it savoury (in China, they tell stories of barbarians who eat meat but no *fan* to frighten their children).

Modern Western society, drunk on meat for the last fifty years, used to polishing off herds of cattle at a single sitting, is starting to re-think. The most recent Canada's

Food Guide to Healthy Eating, for example, advocates five to ten servings of rice and grains a day and five to ten of vegetables and fruit, but you can fulfill the daily meat requirement by eating *two pieces of salami*. That's where I'm trying to lead my family, kicking and screaming, into the next millennium: a rice-based diet.

You can make almost anything into a stir-fry. As you may have noticed, gentlemen, cooking tends to begin with an allium (usually onion, garlic or shallots) simmering in a fat (olive oil, butter or, formerly, lard). Then add in your chopped vegetables, stir, add meat, stir, add spices and seasonings and stir. Then comes a *solvent*: stock, wine or even water. This scoops up whatever tasty residues have stuck to the sides of the pot; and the more you add, the soupier the *ts'ai*. After that is a process of reduction, to concentrate the flavours and thicken the sauce. You can also add a tiny bit of cornstarch or flour, if you wish. Then scoop onto bowls of rice and garnish with cucumber and/or carrot slices— a quick meal. You can plug almost any combination of ingredients into this formula—pork, for example, and green beans, or chicken and broccoli.

Well, that's just a basis. Obviously, you have to keep learning and rotating recipes and growing. It's a great hobby, though, very physical and satisfying. A great vehicle for self-expression in a very Zen way: like making a Zen ice sculpture or sand painting, you pour all this creative energy into it and then it's gone. Often you won't even get a grunt of appreciation. You have to do it for its own sake. And never is that more true than when you have to figure out:

How to Cook for a Baby

After they're weaned, you feed them baby goo, available at most supermarkets or dispensed like a drug from the pharmacy. Remove lid from baby food jar. Spoon into screaming, snot-covered, goo-smeared face. Actually, I've found that reading to Nicholas, holding the book with one hand, spooning the goo with the other, is about the only way to get through mealtimes. In *I'll Be the Parent, You Be the Kid*, Paul Kropp has a whole chapter called "When the kids act up: distraction is not discipline," and he may be right—but I don't care. I'm just trying to preserve my sanity; I'm hanging on by a very thin thread.

How to Cook for a Toddler

Place frozen vegetables, pasta, chicken chunks or leftovers in microwave. Microwave on high, stirring occasionally, until hot. Let cool and serve.

How to Cook for a Kid

At first, I used to take a lot of trouble over cooking for Nicholas; but it was too heartbreaking. I would make him the most delicious dishes, at which he would turn up his retroussé nose in disdain. He'd then gobble down a piece of plain bread. Early on in my househusband career I tried to force him to eat what I wanted him to, but I laugh at those attempts now. Never enter into a battle of wills, into a food fight, with a toddler. You *will* lose. He has superior resources. He'll flay your nerves, frazzle your synapses and stir-fry your sanity. I just try to put healthy things in front of him, figuring if he's hungry, he'll eat. Penelope Leach says kids will select a nutritional diet for themselves over the course of a week, even though "your child may have a bread jag and then a meat passion and then may eat almost nothing but fruit for a day or two." I guess I agree with her, though if it were up to Nicholas, he'd eat nothing but candy, chips and chocolate milk.

Here, by the way, is a recipe Nicholas actually invented:

Broccoli Florets With Applesauce Coulis

Ingredients: applesauce, microwaved broccoli florets

Dip microwaved broccoli floret in applesauce. Lick applesauce off floret. Discard floret.

10. TOWARDS A POSSIBLE REDEFINITION OF MACHISMO

So now I, like my mother before me and her mother before her, cook with one hand (holding Nicholas with the other), eat standing up (who has time to sit?), and pee sitting down (if I do it standing up, Nicholas tries to put his fingers in the stream). Never again, it appears, will I know the almost unseemly pleasure of a peaceful bowel movement. As a bachelor, I might have spent twenty minutes on "the throne," smoking, sipping coffee, reading. Now as soon as I drop my trousers, Nicholas bolts down the hall, and I spend the whole time yelling, "Nicholas! What are you doing? Where are you going? Come back here, please! Nicholas! *Nicholas!*" It's awful.

Every night, I prepare not one but two dinners: one for Nick, one for Pam and me. And when I cook, I wear an apron. Sometimes I worry about the effect seeing me in an apron will have on my son's psyche, recalling the scene in *Rebel Without a Cause* in which the troubled teenager, played by James Dean, finally turns to his father for advice, only to discover him in an apron, doing the dishes. "Oh, no, Dad, how could you?" he says and bolts out of the house to get into even more trouble, into the worst trouble of his life, in fact. The obvious message being: a dad in an apron is a terrible thing.

But were you aware, gentlemen, that while almost all other types of stain can be laundered out of your shirts, grease spots never come out? If hot grease from the stove splatters your shirt, that's the end of your shirt. Yes . . . and I love my shirts too much to treat them with such cavalier disregard. I *love* them. Each shirt is carefully selected from hundreds or perhaps even thousands of highly qualified applicants, for quality, comfort and uniqueness. I will not buy or wear a shirt that is not unique, and therefore I have to treat each the same way a violinist treats a Stradivarius. Do I care more about my shirts than Nicholas's psychological health and need for a strong male role model? Of course not. Nevertheless, I wear an apron when I cook (and I think men can look quite manly in aprons, at least between the hours of 6 and 8 P.M.).

I spend a lot of time in the kitchen. I almost always have a sinkful of soapy water and often a potful of boiling water going at the same time. I mop and sweep, apologizing to

Nicholas the whole time: "I'm sorry, Nicholas. I know this is boring. We'll go to the park as soon as I'm finished. I just have to do this." Sometimes he'll freak out and I'll literally have to *beg* him to let me continue: "Please, Nicholas, please let me mop the floor." I wonder sometimes, how did it come to this? Begging a baby to let me mop the floor feels like karmic backlash, punishment for some sin in a former life or perhaps this one.

Women open doors for *me* now. I'll be wrestling with Nicholas, the stroller, several bottles of wine, perhaps a couple of bags of groceries, trying to open the door with my foot, and some kindly old lady will jump in and say, "Here, let me get that." And she'll stand there holding the door and smiling at me, a huge, strappingly healthy young-ish man. I'm very grateful. It never occurs to men.

I feel naked without a stroller in front of me. . . . In other words, without really meaning to or resorting to any painful or expensive operations, Pam and I have almost completely switched traditional, stereotypical sex-roles. I first noticed this was happening when we started fixing up our old wife-beater's house. "Whew, I hope you're handy," people would say. We weren't, but Pam was learn-ing—talking to hardware store owners, familiarizing her-self with tools, and so on. One Saturday morning, after we had sex, Pam jumped out of bed and started putting on her pants.

"Where are you going?" I asked her.

"I have to phone the hardware store," she said.

The thing was, I wanted to cuddle a bit more. . . . This got me thinking about all the other ways we've switched traditional roles. If we're driving in a car and we get lost, I always want to pull over and ask directions; Pam wants to tough it out with the map. Unlike many men, apparently, I love to shop. I have items all over the city I'll visit against the golden day I can afford them; Pam practically leaves the car running as she dashes into the store and buys a whole season's wardrobe, taking whatever the salesperson recommends.

And, hmmm, let's see, I can't think of . . . Well, I guess there is one other minor, insignificant way we switched things around. It's taken me years of self-administered therapy to be able to admit this: in between cheques for books and magazine gigs, Pam pays me an allowance—although I prefer to think of it as grocery money, since I spend it all on groceries and other family-related items. The only treat I allow myself is the odd espresso while I'm on the road.

The odd shirt, too. As I say, I'm addicted to shirts. Many I buy on sale or second-hand, very cheap. But even then, I always shave a couple of bucks off the price when I tell Pam about it.

"Oh, I see you bought yourself a new shirt," she'll say with a hint of sarcasm in her voice.

"It was a real bargain, only twenty-two dollars," I'll reply, even though the shirt was, in fact, twenty-six dollars.

Such are the pitiful stratagems of the non-earner, or the "dependent," as I'm listed on Pam's tax return. I'm comforted, though, by the thought that in this regard I participate in a rich housewifely tradition. The historian Viviana Zelizer writes that turn-of-the-century, middle-class housewives, for example, "would take change left in their husbands' pockets, have shopkeepers add bogus items to bills and keep the difference, retain money from goods and services produced at home (by renting rooms and sewing, for example), and save money from housekeeping expenses." With working-class families, it was slightly different: the men were paid in cash, in an envelope, and they would usually withhold a certain amount for their own pleasure before turning the rest over to their wives, who often had no idea how much they made.

Shirts, and the odd manual typewriter, which I also can't resist. I've bought so many of them, it's become a sort of de facto hobby. One time, I remember, I spent thirty dollars of grocery money on a beautiful portable Remington, circa 1950. I felt guilty, but I rationalized the expense. It'll pay for itself! I said to myself. I'll leave it lying around the house and type thoughts as they come up. They'll wind up in articles and books. (True, too. Many of the thoughts in this book were typed, in passing, on that same portable manual.) Still, I felt guilty when I thought of all the broccoli, chicken and rice—not to mention fine wines—I could have bought for my family.

"I've got some good news and some bad news," I told Pam when she got home that night. "Or, rather, I have some news you won't be crazy about and a rationalization. Which would you like to hear first?"

"The rationalization, I guess."

"It'll pay for itself!"

"What did you buy?" she asked after a rueful laugh. "Don't tell me another typewriter."

"I'm afraid so."

"I don't believe it. How many typewriters does one man need?" she appealed, as if to the heavens.

"I couldn't help it, Pam. I couldn't resist. It was in such great shape—and such a bargain!"

"How much?" she asked after a pause.

" . . . twenty-five dollars!"

"Oh, well," she sighed. "I guess it could be worse: you could be obsessed with buying something expensive."

"Yeah, like my father. He couldn't stop buying cars. At one point, he had six of them," I reminded her.

And if any man reading this were to say, spitting a stream of tobacco juice into a nearby spittoon, "Househusband? Pushing a stroller, wearing an apron, collecting an allowance from his wife? What a wimp. What a *wuss*. Get a job. Be a *man*. You're embarrassing your entire gender," I would simply say, first of all, I've never been sexier or more attractive to women. Nicholas is a living testimonial, a sandwich board on wheels testifying to the soundness of my genetic structure, the excellent motility of my sperm, and my willingness to commit—all highly attractive qualities to the modern woman, gentlemen. When Nicholas and I stroller into a store or café, we're like a couple of Baldwin brothers. We're mobbed, surrounded by ooh-ing and aah-ing young women. And I've caught women's sneaky, over-the-shoulder looks as I pass in the street—not to check out any aspect of my anatomy, but rather trying to get a peek at what I'm packing in my stroller.

Besides, it's not like I was rustling cattle during my working life. I sat in front of a computer, manipulating information. Whereas now I'm actively involved in bringing Nicholas up from a blob of protoplasm to (I hope) a fine, upstanding young citizen. *¿Quien es mas macho?*

And I'm not sure if you're aware of this, gentlemen, but there's quite a bit of heavy lifting involved in looking after a kid. While you're sitting at your desk, playing Solitaire on your computer or engaged in virtual flirtation via e-mail, we care-providers are busting our butts, humping strollers in and out of streetcars, up and down stairs, over snow-banks and other obstacles. Streetcars are the worst. With sweat trickling down my brow, clutching the handle and front axle of the stroller, I grunt and groan as I try to ma-noeuvre my way around the pole in the middle of the door. Other passengers stand and stare, no doubt thinking, "Wow, that huge, sweaty guy seems to be having a hard time." Through the salty, stinging droplets of sweat in my eyes, I see many women in the same predicament. Mean-while, probably the most strenuous activity their husbands are called upon to perform is to *chew*.

Obviously, it goes against the grain not to be a bread-winner, a provider, the financial supporter of our family. Deep within my DNA lurks the urge to leave the cave in the morning and not return without a bloody carcass slung over my back, or at least something furry and dead on the end of a pointy stick. Every man has this, I believe, but as a man of Norwegian descent I have it twofold, I think. My ancestors scoured the earth, raping and pillaging and chopping people's heads off with battle-axes; I stay home in my apron, and I'm actually thinking of buying a feather duster.

But I can get over it, I think, or at least repress my feel-ings until my New York agent, William, scores me a huge advance, or my Los Angeles agent, Jerry, drops an eye-popping movie-money cheque in my lap. Then, ladies, I will be *the perfect man*: rich and famous, and I change dia-pers, too. It *could* happen. "I've thoroughly explored the bottom of the heap," I'll often say to Pam, in the tone and manner of a university professor or teacher's assistant, "and it's been very interesting, and I feel like I've learned a lot of valuable lessons. However, for me to grow *artistically*, I feel it is time for me to move to the next level. I need a series of surprisingly large cheques or I'm afraid I might stagnate—as an artist."

Pam has a steady job; I have a lottery ticket. She brings home the bacon; I'm going for the whole enchilada. Either I make it, achieve critical mass and *blast off* into the stratosphere, leaving the rest of you suckers in the dust— or I don't. At least I'll have tried. I hope Nicholas will be able to find it in his heart to understand how important it all seemed to me, even when he's frantically applying for scholarships, biting his nails and fretting about his chances.

In the meantime, Pam is a perfectly good provider. I always used to worry vicariously about Pam's job, fretting and fearful lest she get fired. But I don't worry about it so much anymore. Pam's tough, smart and tenacious. At work, she knows when to give in and when to push back. Unlike me, who's always so pathetically grateful to be hired in the first place, they finally have to fire me in disgust. Once, at her office Xmas party, she grabbed her boss's boss, the owner of the station, and bounced him up and down on her hip like he was a baby.

"Oh no, what were you thinking?" I asked her when she told me about it. She's going to get canned for sure, I said to myself and mentally started getting my resumé together. I'll take it to that all-night place and do it myself, I thought. It's cheaper and faster that way. I don't trust those photocopy clerks.

But it turned out Pam's boss's boss liked being bounced on Pam's hip. He said it showed her fun side, under her normally (and I quote) "patrician exterior." He even offered her a promotion, of sorts, a chance to be an entertainment reporter (Pam turned it down; she likes news).

I think it's been good for me, *spiritually*, for Pam to be the breadwinner. I'm far less likely to be tyrannical, peremptory and dismissive and to tick off "logical" points on my fingers. And if I don't get all argumentative, I find, nobody does.

We get along. We joke around about her breadwinner status. If she phones me from work and says she's stressed out, I say, "What's the matter? Stuck on a word in the crossword puzzle? 'Jumble' got you down?" (a reference to my contention that next to looking after a kid, work is pure leisure).

"Very funny, Dave," she'll say. "You're funniest when you've just woken up from your nap."

And here's an interesting point, gentlemen. You can call me a wimp, a wuss and all the rest of it for staying home with a kid, but I am also the least (pardon my language, ladies; I know of no synonyms) pussy-whipped man I know. I can go out with the boys any time I like, on short notice, stagger in at any old hour and nary a peep from Pam. Why? Brownie points, boys. As family chef *and* primary caregiver of Nicholas *and* someone who still earns *some* money, enough at least for various vacations and other luxuries, I have amassed more brownie points than you've had hot dinners. Could it be that I have more brownie points than any man alive? Than any man in history? If brownie points were air miles, I could fly to the moon!

We need to lose the old military models of masculinity, I think, in favour of a peacetime version which hearkens back to the old idea of a gentleman. Manhood should be about sincerity, passion, fidelity and honour. A certain adherence to tradition, perhaps. One of the most manly men I know is probably my college roommate Charles. He's balding, heavy-set and prematurely grey, but he has one of the strongest, most masculine minds I know. A firm and fair-minded lawyer. I'm not sure I'd want him in my foxhole; but if I ran afoul of the law I'd want him to prepare my briefs.

Anyway, since when did money and machismo become so inextricably intertwined? I'd love to return, or move forward, to a time when men derived at least some of their satisfaction not just from earning money but from doing good work—a notion which seems to have become almost completely extinct. Now that the biggest money goes to the most banal pursuits, tough guys in suits bust chops, play power games and establish power bases over movies like *The Stupids* and *Tommy Boy*.

I don't know what happened to me. Maybe it was my mother, whispering to me that I should love what I do and pay no attention to the money. I really took it to heart. I derive most of my satisfaction and sense of male identity from the creation of an oeuvre, something I can point to and be proud of at the end of my life; Numerous recent studies suggest that as many as 80 percent of workers in America find their jobs "meaningless." I'm not surprised: the endless moronic meetings; the back-stabbing, squabbling and butt-covering; and, above all, the sense that for all the frantic effort, busyness and stress, one is producing nothing of any lasting significance or value to humanity. Being a househusband has freed me from all that. Pam has given me the freedom to choose my projects.

"But Dave," you might say, "that's fine for you, but completely unrealistic and quixotic for the rest of us. We have to earn money to pay rent and mortgages."

I understand, although looking around me I see secretaries who should be architects, architects who should be shoe repairmen, barbers who should be bankers, authors who should be agents. It's just a matter of courage to quit the job you have to seek something more suitable. There are many ways to earn a living, and you'd probably earn more doing something you love, because you'd be good at it. Just imagine how beautiful this world would be if everyone loved what they did. This is an idea I was trying out over the phone recently, on my friend Jill, shamelessly workshopping material on her.

"Just imagine how beautiful the world would be if everyone cared about what they did," I said. "Imagine how beautiful houses would be if people loved building them. Imagine how beautiful shoes would be if the people who made them really loved making them—"

"My shoes *are* beautiful, Dave," she retorted.

So maybe I'm wrong. I usually am. Probably the real truth is that because of my size and strength, I've never really worried about coming off as macho; so being a househusband is unembarrassing to me (part of why I don't mind writing this book: I'm secure enough to do so). I'm a naturally manly, virile man—a fact of which I'm having to remind Pam with increasing frequency of late, I'm forced to say. Recently, Pam and I went to see our friend Helene starring in a small-theatre production of *Medea* on opening night. I went to great pains to look good, slapped on a flash suit and performed my toilette with even more than usual care. I was ready about an hour early, so while we were waiting for the babysitter to arrive, I lounged around the living room in various poses and attitudes—but not a peep from Pam. Finally, worn out by her indifference, I asked her, "So what do you think?"

"Of what?"

"How do I look?"

"Oh, um, yes. Nice."

"Nice? Pam, you may have forgotten, but I am a handsome, virile man. You've just lost all appreciation for that fact."

"Oh, yes, I'm sorry, Dave," she said, seeming genuinely stricken, which mollified me somewhat. "You are. Don't I tell you that quite often?"

"Not often enough," I said sulkily, allowing her to hug me. Then, on our way out, I noticed on my wrist, where a watch should have been, a rubber band. . . . The time has come, I suppose, to set aside youthful vanity. "My days of love are over;" as Byron wrote at age thirty, "me no more/The charms of maid, wife, and still less of widow,/ Can make the fool of which they made before." With no small measure of regret, and long before I'm ready, I have to relinquish leading-man status. I'm the sidekick now, a wisecracking character actor: Salty, the wise old sea-salt; or in my case, perhaps even Punchy, the punch-drunk rodeo clown. Oh well, it's a relief, really. It's just not about me any more; I can relax.

Sometimes I think I'm actually a good role model for Nicholas. He sees me perform a variety of activities in a big gender-neutral mush: fax documents, talk to my agent, shave, do the dishes, polish my shoes, type, lift weights, make a tuna fish sandwich, write. He knocks on my office door, comes in, crawls on my lap and starts tapping away at the keyboard.

"I'm writer!" he'll say, which naturally causes the valves and ventricles of my ticker to fibrillate with joy—and anxiety.

"It's a terrible way to try to make a living," I'll tell him. He doesn't care. He keeps tapping away. "What are you writing about?" I ask him.

"Baseball player," he invariably responds.

He sees his father at work, which is something a lot of kids don't get. But *they* are the historical anomaly. Don't forget, it's only been the last 150 years or so men have been leaving the house en masse to earn a living. Before the Industrial Revolution, all industry was pretty much what we call a "cottage industry" today, and sons learned their trades from watching their fathers work at them. True, Nicholas only gets a faint glimmer of that, and I have to shut my door in his face to get anything done, but at least he gets a sense of it; I do not simply vanish in the morning and reappear at night. And I produce a tangible product: he can see me going over my manuscripts, tearing out my hair, and decide whether that's something he'd like to do, or not.

I wish I could say I derive more manly satisfaction from looking after this house. Sometimes I feel a faint glimmer of machismo from rolling up my sleeves and really giving the kitchen floor a good scrub, say. There's a pleasant sense of restoring order, or at least of keeping the dogs of chaos at bay. As Neil Postman says in *The End of Education*, "Every time we clean our homes . . . we are combating entropy, using intelligence and energy to overcome (that is, postpone) the inevitable decay of organization." (Only Neil Postman could have such a lofty theory about housework; kind of makes you wonder how much of it he actually does.) Other times, I try to think of housework as an exercise in monk-like humility: "Every day, he got up and scrubbed and swept his cell." Other times—

and here is perhaps where I cross the line into pathos—I approach it as *exercise*. All that bending and stretching, don't you know. I do it at top speed, sometimes donning shorts and a T-shirt, trying to work up a sweat.

Mostly, though, I feel . . . nothing. When it comes to household matters, I'm less like Neil Postman and more like Charles Bukowski, who once, in a drunken stupor, lunged at some woman in his apartment but lost his footing and belly-flopped on his coffee table, flattening it. He left it like that for months, flattened on the floor. If anyone asked him why he didn't fix it, or get a new one, he'd say, "I like it like that."

The bottom line, probably, is that I derive most of whatever sense of machismo I have from my skills as a writer. I look at it like this: writers have always needed something to do in the afternoons to take their minds off writing. Hemingway had the bulls; Bukowski had the track; I change diapers and push a stroller around.

But I'm just a transitional figure, ladies. Maybe someday men will brag and boast to each other about how quickly they can change a diaper, or what great baby-burpers they are. . . . I *do* take a certain amount of manly pride in my fidelity to Pam; and someday I'd like to write a book called *Tropic of Monogamy* or something that attempts to do for monogamy what Henry Miller did for infidelity and promiscuity—make it sound like an adventure. Which is what it is: a real high-wire act. Anyone can cheat or leave, but it takes balls to stick around. Or so I'd argue in *Tropic of Monogamy*, anyway.

In this age of fatherlessness (in the United States, about 40 percent of children live in homes without fathers, compared to 17 percent in 1960; soon it could be around 50 percent), the simple act of being a dad who has stuck around feels pretty butch—although here again the bread-winner question rears its head. What if Pam didn't earn money? How responsible would I seem then? But she does, and anyway I like to think I could still, with a fantastic, superhuman effort, land a job, maybe as an advertising copywriter—or the job my friend Max held for a long time, writing in-house skits for corporate getaways, making gentle, flattering fun of the boss and other office characters, while savagely, viciously satirizing the competition. And with the enhanced incentive of having a family to feed, I could keep the job this time, hold it down like a bad oyster.

We're in this together. We're *partners*. I used to object to being called Pam's "partner" because it felt too businesslike. Are we married or launching a new line of perfume? But now I've decided I don't mind it. We're more than partners, but we *are* partners, an effective and affective political and economic unit. When I was single, it was me versus the world. Now it's us versus the world, and for the first time I think I might just have a chance.

Anyway, we haven't completely switched roles yet. Pam's not like a typical 1950s dad. She doesn't come home and hide behind the paper. She can't wait to see Nicholas; she's missed him. The minute she comes through the door, she takes over. It's a real relief. I can't fathom what it would be like to have to look after him all the time, all by myself, without her help and support, as women have had to do since the dawn of time; I'd go out of my mind. I've even seen a study, by Dr. Kyle Pruett of the Yale Child Study Center, that suggests kids with stay-at-home dads are better off than other kids, because they get attention from *both* parents; whereas in traditional stay-at-home-mom households, dads tend to remain remote figures.

Meanwhile, as I've said, I'm naturally ambitious, so I'm unlikely simply to allow myself to fall into the home-maker's role; whereas Pam might, she admits, if she stayed home and I earned the money.

Other times, though, it does feel like we really have switched roles and I'm an old-fashioned 1950s housewife. Pam will come home, in a black mood because of some-thing that happened at work that day, then calm down when she sniffs the air and smells the delicious roast I've got cooking in the oven. Proudly I scamper into the kitchen, apron-clad, mix up two ultra-dry Gibsons in my old-fashioned shaker (a present from Pam for my first Father's Day), take two frosted, infundibuliform glasses out of the freezer, pour the drinks, put them on a tray, bring them out into the living room, where Pam is massag-ing her sore feet, slide the cocktails under her nose and say, "How was your day, dear?"

11. "WHAT DO YOU *DO* ALL DAY?"

Now, not only do I have to answer the omnipresent question *What do you do?* but the even more impertinent and ill-bred follow-up, *What do you do all day?* (When we're alone together, out of earshot, we homemakers will quietly and compassionately ask each other, "What *did* you do?" And the follow-up is usually "Do you think you'll go back to it?")

"What do you *do* all day?" I've been searching for a snappy, quippy answer to this question, but I haven't found one yet. I was heartened to read an article recently by one Meghan Cox Gurdon, of Washington, D.C., in the *Women's Quarterly.* She's one of the "new" housewives: "She could have made partner but she chucked it all to move to the suburbs to have kids." She loves staying at

home with her kids. In the article, she talks about her surprise—not to mention the surprise of her feminist
mother—at finding herself happy in the role of stay-at-
home mom. The accompanying illustration shows her
standing proudly in front of Diaper World with a kid in
one hand and a baby in a car seat in the other, wearing a superhero outfit with the letter M emblazoned on it.

But she doesn't know how to deal with this question
either, which she calls "the one dinner-party query that
leaves all but the most self-assured gasping like beached
tuna." She lists a variety of possible responses: 1) past
tense: "I'm—er, I used to be a diplomat/lawyer/fill-in-the-
blank"; 2) apologetic: "I'm just a stay-at-home mom"; 3)
effervescent: 'What do I do?' (Tinkly laughter.) 'Whatever
I like. What do *you* do?'

But I don't really do "tinkly laughter." Mostly I just
stand there, stumped, flummoxed, cretinized, wondering
whatever happened to the old-world values of discretion,
courtesy and restraint.

Pam's asked me this question on a couple of occasions,
occasions when she comes home and the house is a mess and
Nicholas is filthy, his face smeared with chocolate and dirt,
his sodden, urine-saturated diaper hanging down around
his knees, and me with no plans for dinner, muttering only,
"Pizza—you pay" through parched lips before keeling over
in a dead faint, figuring, "Hey, he's uninjured. I've done my
job. I 'fathered' him all day. Now I say 'uncle.'"

"Dave," Pam said to me on one of these occasions, "you
know, as a househusband you're supposed to tidy up the
house. But it's actually messier when I come home than
when I leave." And then she dropped it on me: "What do
you *do* all day?"

"You want to know what I do all day? I'll tell you what I do," I said. "Nicholas chases the cat from room to room, and I chase him. Each room we enter he tries to tear apart, and I try to tidy it up. If I manage to take a break even, I consider myself lucky. After that, we'll get some groceries, and then it's time for lunch. When he naps, I nap. Then we go to the park, and after arguing with him for half an hour I finally get him to come home to have some dinner, and that's when, when the house's mess is at its absolute zenith, or nadir, you come storming in, in your suit and high heels, demanding to know what I do all day."

"Dave, I keep telling you, you have to clean up as you go along," she said.

Of course I agree with her, and I acknowledge the house could be tidier. But, I repeat, I'm just a transitional figure. Perhaps someday, there will emerge from the primordial stew an *Überhausmensch* who can not only look after a kid and maintain some semblance of a career but also keep his house tidy and clean. But until then I'm doing the best I can.

I've even had a journalism student follow me around all day, trying to figure out the answer to the puzzling, consternating question of how I spend my time. Her name was Shawna. One day, not too long after *Chump Change* hit the bookstores, she phoned me out of the blue.

"I want to follow you around on a typical day," she explained over the phone. "It's part of my school's job-shadowing program?"

"But I don't *have* a job," I told her.

"That doesn't matter. I just want to tag along and see what you do on a typical day."

"I don't do *anything* on a typical day." She laughed. She

thought I was joking. "I'm serious," I told her. "Some days I don't even leave the house. Following me around would be the most boring thing you have ever done in your life."

But she persisted, and she sounded kind of sexy, in a perky, internish way, so in the end I said OK. I told her I write in the morning, so she could come over at noon. She came. Since I couldn't think of anything else to do with her, we went shopping for fruit in Kensington Market (with Nicholas, naturally) and grabbed a cheapo Chinese lunch special. I talked a blue streak the entire time, trying to stave off the inevitable conclusion that my life was boring beyond redemption, but she *claimed* to be green with envy. "I want your life!" she kept saying, like a cheerful, bubbly Dracula. (She was kind of cute, and I liked having someone following me around all day. I wish it happened more often.)

So, since there's such intense curiosity out there about this topic, here, for the illumination of all and sundry, is a description of

A Typical Day

Begins early, like a farmer's. And it begins with a question: Nicholas standing up in his crib, rattling the bars and calling out, "Mommy? Daddy? Mommy? Daddy?"

I squint at my watch: 6:18 A.M. I feel . . . dreadful. It's a little-known fact of parenthood that you drink more than ever. At least Pam and I do. "Booze is the grease that keeps our relationship running smoothly," I tell people. "For God's sake, don't attempt parenthood without incredible amounts of booze." They should sell bottles of Scotch and wine at the drugstore, right next to the diapers and wipes.

But the mornings are hell. I've never been a morning person. I'm not even sure I'm a full-fledged person before about ten. I'm probably more of a crustacean, one of the lower invertebrates. It takes about twenty cups of coffee to get me going. My brain is like one of those room-filling 1956 Univac computers, all vacuum tubes and reel-to-reel tape-decks, the kind you program using cards with holes punched in them. It takes about three hours to boot up in the morning, and is likewise very difficult to power down at night; you might need to use a pipe wrench.

"We have to go to bed early tonight," Pam and I say to each other every morning, but almost never do. The time after Nicholas goes to bed is almost the only time we have to ourselves. After a day of drudgery and diapers (me) or chasing after interviews in a huge sport-utility vehicle with her cameraman (Pam), are we just going to have dinner, do the dishes and crash? I don't think so. I know a few people who have gone this route—or rather, I *used* to know them. They have a kid, and poof!—disappear from sight, drop off the social radar, bubble under the waves, glub-glub-glub. You don't hear from them anymore; they stop returning your calls, and everyone else's. Maybe after six months or a year, you get a guilty, haunted call from one of these underwater parents, a message saying, "Hi, sorry I didn't call you back. We should get together sometime." Beeep! But they never materialize on the physical plane, they remain forevermore a disembodied voice on the other end of a phone.

I can't let that be my fate. Socializing has always been extremely important to me—even if, more than once lately, I've sat staring into space with nothing to say. Still! I love mixing and mingling, and I consider everything good that's ever happened to me to be the direct or indirect result of socializing. My family, career, this house: all a product of socializing, of spending time with the people who share my time on this earth.

"Mommy? Daddy? Mommy? Daddy?"

Still Pam and I lie there, moaning and groaning like a couple of tortured animals. As time passes and neither of us gets up, Nicholas's question takes on a moral, even a political, flavour. Thirty years ago, perhaps, it wouldn't have been a question at all. Nicholas, standing up and rattling the bars of his crib, would have framed his comments in the form of a straightforward declarative statement: "Mommy!" But times have changed, and now it's a question. Mommy? Daddy? Which one of you is coming down to get me, and how do you arrive at that decision? What criteria do you use?

I have to be honest here. Four or even five and sometimes six mornings out of seven, Pam is the one to drag her carcass out of bed and go get him, while I roll over with a grunt of relief and put the pillow over my head. Why? How do I justify this inequity? I don't. I'm trying to improve in this department; it's just that self-improvement is so difficult at that time of the morning. Lately, Pam has been taking the bull by the horns and saying, "Dave? You want to get him this morning?"

"Oh, sure," I'll say, as if that were my intention all along. I roll out of bed as if on two stumps (I don't know if it's poor circulation or whether I've finally succumbed to the gout or some other nineteenth-century disease, but lately I can barely feel my feet when I get out of bed in the morning) to fetch Nicholas from his crib. Moral quandary number two is deciding whether to take him back upstairs to our bed, or downstairs to the living room. If I take him upstairs, neither of us will get any more sleep. We always think we will, but he thrashes around, kicks us in the ribs, and squirts juice on us until we wake up. The other alternative is to take him downstairs and lie on the couch while he watches television and munches on no-name O-shaped oat cereal, dry. That's the noble option, because it allows Pam to get some richly deserved sleep.

It doesn't feel that noble, though, when Nicholas's favourite television program, *Teletubbies*, an import from Britain—the land that produced Chaucer, Shakespeare, and Milton—comes on. When I first read about the advent of this show in the newspapers, I swore I'd never let Nicholas watch it. Lying on the couch, with a pillow over my face and Nicholas sitting on my stomach, I hear the theme song kick in: "Tinky Winky! Dipsy! Laa-Laa! Po!"

Tinky Winky, Dipsy, Laa-Laa and Po are the Teletubbies, fuzzy, pear-shaped creatures with antennae on their heads and television monitors on their stomachs. Pam says they're supposed to be aliens. They live in an Astroturf-covered dome in the middle of a weird golf-course-like landscape, on which rabbits the size of schnauzers (specially bred for the show, I read somewhere) graze placidly. The landscape is dotted with windmills, and when the windmills turn, the Teletubbies jump up and down with joy and gather together. Their antennae glow, then one of them is "chosen" and his/her (two are male, two are female, though for some reason one of the male Teletubbies carries a purse) tummy glows and plays a five- or six- or even seven-minute segment of some kid-friendly activity, like brushing a horse or riding around on a tricycle. Then, when it's over, all the other Teletubbies laugh and clap and say "again! again!" and the whole segment plays *again*.

The whole thing is deeply weird. I've heard that the Teletubbies are a cult hit among rave kids in England. When they return to their parents' houses at dawn after being up all night at a rave, they'll flip on *Teletubbies* before they crash. I'm not surprised. The whole thing is like an ecstasy flashback, if there is such a thing.

But what bothers me most about the show is the complete lack of parental figures in the Teletubbies' Orwellian/Huxleyan world. Their Astroturf-covered dome/home has doors that open and shut automatically, like the doors at a supermarket, and is cleaned by a robot vacuum cleaner with eyes (his nose is the hose). When they're hungry, they eat none-too-nutritious-looking Tubby Custard and Tubby Toast, which they dispense to themselves by pressing a button on one of two elaborate, Rube Goldberg-esque machines (they're so young that they talk toddlerish gibberish, yet they operate all this heavy machinery). Every once in a while, a kind of periscope/ loudspeaker rises from the ground with a loud noise of machinery and gives them instructions on various activities, almost all of which are recreational in nature. The action is presided over by a smiling, squealing live-action toddler's face in an animated sun. What are the producers of *Teletubbies* saying here? That the toddler is God?

I should turn it off, obviously, but I don't. Nicholas sits on my stomach, staring with pinwheel eyes at his beloved Teletubbies, while I lie on the couch like a sick frog. It's my second moral defeat of the day (the first was not springing up to get him), and it isn't even eight o'clock. I'm losing the battle against the juggernaut, I'm abrogating my responsibility as a parent, I'm in passive collusion with "the Man," with "the Machine," but what can I do? I'm just one man, and I'm so, so tired. . . . The only straw I clutch at is this: at least it's public television. No commercials.

I wage a huge battle with myself, lying on the couch. A strictly internal battle; if you saw me lying there, you might be tempted to take my pulse. Other shows come on, like *Bookmice*. ("Bookmice! Look twice! They live in the stacks of the li-bra-ree-ee. . . .") That show probably encourages reading, I think, lying there like a corpse. Once in a while I'll rouse myself to squint myopically at the screen, mostly thinking, what sort of career tragedy led these actors and other performers to wind up on a kiddie show? Many of them are middle-aged. Every once in a while you'll even see a half-familiar face. Who do you have to piss off to wind up as a grumpy tree on a show about a friendly dragon? I imagine these actors on the phone to their agents every day, saying, "Man, this grumpy tree gig is killing me! Has *anything else* come up? Did you ever hear back from the Quickie Muffler people? What about that minivan commercial? Am I still up for that?"

One show features a folk trio called Sharon, Lois & Bram. Every once in a while they burst into song, and you see copies of their incredibly dated-looking albums fly past in the background. What happened to them? Did they fail to move with the times, to go electric along with everyone else? When all the other folkies were plugging in, did they stick to their guns? Are they now kicking themselves and phoning their agents in between takes?

These and other equally terrifying questions finally cattle-prod me off the couch. I jump up, setting Nicholas aside, and head to the kitchen where I make myself some really strong coffee, muttering, "I've got to get *cracking*. From now on I have to jump out of bed at the crack of dawn and hit the ground running!" The sight of those hokey folkies has given me the heebie-jeebies. I have a couple of actor friends. I hope I never see either of them wind up as an avuncular buddy to a hand-puppet on one of those shows. It'd be like . . . seeing a friend in a gay porn movie.

I make the coffee, and some juice and toast for Nicholas. Like all kids, he is crazy for juice and drinks it constantly. Probably smart. Sometimes I'll even squeeze the juice fresh; kids need all the fresh, healthy stuff they can get, and I'm always stuffing him with fruit slices, veggie sticks and chicken strips. After that, if it's one of the mornings when Audrey comes over, I'll go up and get dressed. It wouldn't do to greet her in my pyjamas, although I have on a couple of occasions. On the days she isn't coming, I'll remain in my pyjamas and bathrobe until something I'm reading, or something someone says on the phone, inspires me to choose an outfit for that day.

While Audrey looks after Nicholas, I try to get some writing done. It's tough. Nicholas knows I'm up here, and whenever he can get away from Audrey he makes a beeline for my office. "Knock, knock," he'll say, and then I hear a knock on the door. Can I deny him entry? I'd have to have a heart of stone. I open the door, he charges in, and from that point on it's a battle. He wants to fool around with everything, especially my computer. Finally Audrey comes in to drag him out, which is another battle, possibly ending in tears.

Has any writer in history ever had such distractions? I sometimes wonder. Did Orwell have to deal with anything like this? What about H.L. Mencken? Just as I'm thinking this, Pam sashays by, fresh out of the tub, on her way up the stairs, wearing only a towel—on her head.

At noonish, Audrey or I will feed Nicholas lunch. Frankly, I prefer it if Audrey does. I hate battling with him over food. Pam and I have different philosophies over this. She'll sit there for forty-five minutes reading him stories, pretending the spoon is a plane or boat, pleading with him to eat. I figure if he's hungry, he'll eat.

After lunch, I read Nicholas a couple of stories and he hits the hay. Reading Nicholas a lot of stories is the cornerstone of my self-justification as a stay-at-home dad. Maybe I am an overgrown babysitter; maybe, rather than have me stay home with him and write, he'd prefer to have me go to work, earn sixty thousand a year and put it all towards his college education. But at least I read to him a lot. He'll be so smart he can get a scholarship—if such things still exist when he goes to university.

After the last story, I put him to bed and give him his "lipsticks," without which he can't, or won't, go to sleep. If we were to go on a trip and forget these, it would be a disaster. Empty, hollowed-out lipstick containers are his "transitional objects." They help him make the transition from having a parent around to being on his own; he puts one on each finger, like Edward Lipstickhands. Then I give him his "bubba," his pacifier, pull the blinds and tell him I love him. Before he goes to sleep, Nicholas likes to know he's loved. Who doesn't?

"Have a nice nap, Nick," I'll say.

"Lie down few minutes, Daddy?" he'll say then.

"All right, kiddo."

This is the highlight of the faceless drudge's day: stretching out next to Nick, waiting for him to finish thrashing around and subside into sleep. I love watching his eyes flicker, then close; his little cherub face at peace in sleep. While he sleeps, I lie next to him in the dark, listening to him breathe, letting all kinds of crazy thoughts pop into my head. Stretched out like this, relaxed, horizontal, I do my best thinking, solve numerous nagging problems, I find—because I'm not trying.

Meanwhile, Nicholas is rapidly going through the gears, shifting into deeper and deeper phases of sleep. Sometimes I find myself envious of whatever dopamine or other chemical it is that allows Nicholas to sleep through almost any noise. The construction rages on next door, huge cement mixers and jackhammers fire up, but nothing wakes him up. Once he's settled into deep-sleep mode, a jumbo jet could shear off the tops of all the houses on our block and crash-land in our backyard, and still he wouldn't wake up.

After he falls asleep, I go downstairs, stretch out on the couch and read until sleep takes *me*. Wouldn't this be a good time, you might ask, to catch up on the household chores, to sweep the kitchen floor and mop it, whisk the dust-bunnies off the stairs, spritz the windows with a little window-cleaner and wipe them off with the squeegee you bought to motivate yourself to clean all the windows and which now sits covered in dust in the basement, and the one million other things you've told us you neglect, Dave, and which make you a terrible housekeeper?

It's true I could do all these things and more. But I don't, and I don't feel guilty, either. I did before, but now I don't. I have made my peace with the dust-devils of house-keeping. "When my youngest child started kindergarten," Margie Rutledge wrote in *The Globe and Mail* recently, in an article about motherhood and writing that six people told me I should read, "I made the decision not to do anything while my children were out of the house that I could do while they were at home. Of course that's easier said than done. But I do try not to cook, clean or shop, even if the house is messy and meals are haphazard sometimes. I sit. And sometimes I write."

Exactly. I sit. And sometimes I stretch out on the couch and read. I can't cheerfully declare, as some parents do, "I never read a book now!" I need to read; it's part of my profession and also sustains my soul. The time I spend stretched out horizontal on the couch is "personal and professional development time." The main reason I read is not for entertainment or information, but to see if there's anyone out there with a similar sensibility to mine. I haven't found many, but the few I've found keep me going, make me feel like less of an oddball, or freak. I've read for the same reason since I was fourteen.

Maybe an hour later, the phone will startle me out of my "personal and professional development time." I'll sit up with a start, dab the drool off my cheek with a handkerchief, swing my feet onto the floor and grab the phone. I'll talk to whomever it is—a magazine editor, say, or a friend who doesn't have much to do at work and no one looking over his/her shoulder. Afterwards I'll do a little light drudgery, some curls or sit-ups in my office or some revision on the computer. Sometimes, though, Nicholas will wake up in the middle of my phone call. "Mommy? Daddy?"

"It's me, Nicholas," I'll say, entering his darkened room. "It's your dad."

"Mommy cab-work?" he'll ask, meaning: Is Mommy still at work? He calls work "cab-work" because she takes a cab to work every morning. She used to take the streetcar, but lately she's been getting death threats—someone with nothing better to do has been writing her nasty letters from his (no doubt) dank basement apartment or the rec room of his mother's house—and so now, to be on the safe side, her station's given her an unlimited stack of cab chits.

"Yes, Nicholas," I'll whisper to him in the crepuscular semi-darkness of his room. "Your mommy took a cab, and now she's at work. But Daddy's here. How's that? Is that any good?"

"No!" Nicholas used to say, for the longest time. "No good!" he'd elaborate. "Mommy! Mommy! Mommy!" This is the nadir of the faceless drudge's day, when I invariably think, "What am I doing? Breaking the bond between mother and son? Madness! A connection that goes that deep should never be messed with!"

Lately though, believe it or not, when I say, "Daddy's here. How about that? Will that do?" he says, "Daddy here!" and throws his arms around my neck. Do I need to describe my feelings at such a moment? A complex emotional cocktail, but if it were a martini, *relief* would be the gin, if you see what I'm saying. Then, with Nicholas's head resting sleepily on my shoulder, we'll head into my office and kick back on my reclining chair until he de-groggifies. I enjoy these mellow moments: my little boy curled up on my stomach, his tiny hand, perhaps, on my chest, radiating warmth. I can feel the warmth through my shirt. If it's chilly in my office, I'll throw my favourite sweater over us, a curling sweater as heavy as a horse blanket, with a picture of a rock and two brooms on the back. Or if someone's on the phone, I'll hand it to him, saying, "It's [whomever]. You want to say hi?"

"Hello . . . sandbox . . . bye-bye!" he'll say, pausing for a long time between each word and breathing heavily into the receiver.

If it's not summer, or the weather's lousy, I'll take him to the drop-in centre. On the wall are various pamphlets with titles like *Battle at Bedtime Can Give Baby Tooth Problems* and *Can I Get My Job Back if I Am Fired?* (Inside, like a Christmas card, is the answer or punchline: "Usually you cannot get your job back if you are fired. . . .") On the wall, framed and laminated, laser-printed from someone's computer, is "The Toddler's Creed":

> If I want it, it's mine.
> If I give it to you and change
> my mind later, it's mine.
> If I can take it away from you,
> it's mine.
> If I had it a little while ago,
> it's mine.
> If it's mine, it will never belong to
> anybody else, no matter what.
> If we are building something
> together, all the pieces are mine.
> If it looks just like mine, it is
> mine.

"Toddler's Creed," indeed. Most people practise those principles well into a ripe old age. Unfortunately for Nicholas, though, he's inherited my disaffected philosopher's temperament, along with his mother's kindness and generosity. If another kid grabs a toy from him, Nicholas just stares at him (it's usually a boy), with a look on his face that says, "Why didn't you tell me you wanted it that badly? I would've given it to you."

I don't know what the other nannies, grannies and mommies at the drop-in think of me, a huge, goateed, be-spectacled man in army pants and platinum blond, spiky hair. I'm usually the only man who comes to the drop-in centre. One other dad came once, but I think it was just a day off for him, and he spent the whole time taking pictures of his kid. I do see quite a few guys at the park on weekdays, but they don't come to the drop-in much.

Mostly the grannies, nannies and mommies leave me alone, which is fine. I don't particularly want to gossip about neighbourhood affairs or exchange tips about baby food. I don't want to get into parental politics any more than work politics. That would be jumping out of the frying pan and into the fire, as far as I'm concerned; although if I overhear them talking about school I prick up my ears and maybe even jot down things they say in my notebook. Mostly, I sit and read in the corner, and they ignore me.

"That's that girl Pam's boy," I overheard one woman tell her friend once.

"You know her, the one that's on TV?"

"Oh, yes, he looks just like her."

I, a mere writer, am invisible to them, a blob. No matter how famous I become, even if I win the Nobel Prize, my name will mean nothing to them, my books will probably never appear on their bookshelves—whereas Pam's image flickers on their faces almost every night. All praise and bow down to the Almighty Tube!

I am pretty isolated. House*wives* complain about loneliness and isolation; imagine what it must be like to be a househusband. As garrulous and sociable as I am at night,

I avoid people as much as possible during the day. A strange misanthropy comes over me, and all I want is to be alone (with Nicholas). "Do I contradict myself?/ Very well then I contradict myself," as Walt Whitman wrote. We were meant to be that way, I feel: the night was made for socializing, the day for reflection, apologies and atonement.

I like being alone during the day. If there is, indeed, a force shaping the events of my life, then I believe the main purpose of that radio gig was to put the book *Hermits* in my hand, the very book that helped get me canned. I've read and reread that book; it's like a bible to me now. It's the perfect book for a househusband career. It offers the one thing only books have ever been able to offer me, *la consolation des arts*.

Of special interest to me is the chapter called "Ornamental Hermits: an Interlude." In the eighteenth century, it was fashionable to be sociable, a city dweller. "When a man is tired of London, he is tired of life," as Samuel Johnson famously declared. You had to be up on the latest painters, on the scene at the theatre to applaud the latest Oliver Goldsmith or Richard Sheridan satire. But there was also a conflicting fashion to be melancholy and "deep," to put it about that one spent a certain amount of time on the mountaintop, metaphorical or actual, pondering the eternal verities. "There was a way out of this impasse for the men of means," Peter France writes. "Since they believed there is no point in doing anything for yourself if you can pay somebody to do it for you, they employed people to be melancholy on their behalf."

These "ornamental hermits" had a vogue from the middle of the eighteenth century to the end of the nineteenth. Wealthy men would advertise in the newspaper for someone to live rent-free in a specially constructed grotto or hermitage on their estates. In exchange, all they had to do was take a vow of silence and solitude and act the role of hermit. For example, in the late 1700s, a certain Mr. Powys of Marcham advertised "a reward of 50 pounds a year for life to any man who would undertake to live seven years under ground without seeing anything human; and to let toe and finger nails grow with his hair and beard, during the whole time." In return, Mr. Powys promised quarters that were "very commodious, with a cold bath, a chamber organ, as many books as the occupier pleased, and provisions served from his own table." (It never occurred to Mr. Powys that, as someone else put it, "a hermit who takes a newspaper is not a hermit in whom one can have complete confidence.") He had several takers, but no one lasted more than four years, apparently.

So: I am Pam's "ornamental hermit." A status symbol. She can afford me, I contemplate the meaning of the universe on her behalf, and meanwhile spend my time alone—except for Nicholas, of course. I push him all over the city, my mind on other things, although lately he's been interrupting my inner monologues a lot with his comments. People have even been coming to me for advice recently, thinking my solitude must confer some sort of wisdom on me. My friend Doug, he of the fateful book launch party, was at a crossroads recently. He couldn't decide whether to take a job he'd been offered in advertising or go think things over at a Zen retreat specializing in manual labour in New Mexico. For something like four hundred dollars a week, they get you to scrub floors, wash walls, farm, etc., all in the name of enlightenment.

"Which do you think I should do, Dave?"

"Why don't you stay here at our house for a couple of weeks, Doug?" I asked him. "I have a lot of enlightening chores you could do."

"Come on, seriously, Dave."

"Doug, I'm hardly the guy to give out career advice. Sometimes I spend the whole day in my bathrobe and slippers."

"Dave, that's exactly who *should* give career advice."

In the end, he wound up going to the Zen manual-labour camp. He lasted two days. "They put me on a tractor, Dave," he explained. (*That* I would have paid good money to see, my chrome-domed, Jewish, urban, novelist friend Doug bouncing around on a tractor on some god-forsaken patch of land in New Mexico. *I* would have paid four hundred dollars a week just to observe that; it would have done my soul great good.)

If it's summer and a nice day, I grab Nicholas's shovel and pail, an extra diaper, some juice, a banana, some cookies, a book and a pen and notebook, and we head to the park and his beloved sandbox. While he plays, I may make some notes and/or turn a few precious pages of whatever I'm reading. My theory is that the sandbox is the precursor to television, in the sense that it keeps kids occupied for long periods of time so you can pursue your own agenda; except the sandbox, a hot, dusty crucible in which he learns many truths about greed, indifference, selfishness and shallowness—human nature, in other words—has to be better for Nicholas's development as a human being. Sitting on the edge of the sandbox, I also hope he'll learn that the toys themselves are not important, but what you do to get them. The toy trucks, the shovels, the plastic pails—he wants them so badly, I can see it in his eyes. Nicholas is one of nature's gentlemen; he doesn't grab, although he does wrestle with the urge, I can tell. If a kid is playing with a cool truck or something else he wants, he just stands next to the kid and stares, hoping the kid will offer it (rare, but it happens).

Later, though, of course, neither of them will care about the truck; they'll want something else. Sometimes, seeing him play, his gentleness, I wonder if he isn't aware of this, if in his dealings with other kids he isn't thinking, "Soon this toy truck will be meaningless to both of us. What's important is how we treat one another." Probably not. But as I sit on the edge of the sandbox, watching him play, it certainly occurs to me. It also occurs to me that if there is a God looking down upon our earthly antics, God is probably thinking something similar. We chase after things, throw tantrums, are irrational and constantly demand treats, toys and presents. God wonders when we'll grow up, but loves us despite everything and finds our antics (mostly) charming. It seems pretty obvious, doesn't it? God is a parent.

Nicholas isn't a complete milquetoast/doormat. I should mention that he doesn't like it if another kid grabs a toy he's playing with, and he is capable of putting up quite a fuss, holding onto the toy with all his might, digging his heels into the sand and screaming. On these occasions I may have to intervene—always a ticklish situation: you could offend the other child's parent. Sandbox etiquette dictates that the parent or guardian of the offending child step in, but they're often knitting or reading or chatting, or in some other way not paying attention. So you may actually have to discipline someone else's child. In *Miss Manners' Guide to Rearing Perfect Children*, Judith Martin suggests that in a situation like that, you "feign interest in the child's safety and say, while grabbing the child's wrist, 'I wouldn't do that, dear, because you might get hurt.' It is the invisible pressure on the wrist that suggests to the child the source of that hurt."

But that seems unnecessarily severe to me. An adult doesn't need to threaten a child with violence; one's very size and weight are in themselves an implicit threat. My favoured method is to gently separate the two, while naturally ruling in favour of my child as to the cause of that dispute. "Here, Nick, you take the truck." And perhaps to hunker down on my haunches, bring my big, round, stubbly face close to the other kid's, and say, "Don't take his toys from him." Unfair? Perhaps. But objectivity is not among my attributes when it comes to Nicholas.

Let's say it's a spring day and dusk begins around five o'clock. Dusk, the time when everyone goes to the park to walk whatever they've got: kids, dogs, the occasional ferret. (Dogs are an obvious child substitute, in my opinion, and people tell me they're almost as much work. Soon enough, Nicholas will want one of these vile beasts for himself, but I'm going to wait until he's old enough to beg.) I start warning Nicholas it's time to go home. "Two more trips down the slide, Nicholas, then we have to go."

"No! Free! Four!" he'll say, having already learned the rudiments of negotiation. After the agreed-upon three or four trips down the slide, I'll say, "OK, time to go. *Now*, Nicholas," at which point he'll turn his melting-est gaze upon me, his father, and plead for one more. I can never resist, although I'm trying to be a stern disciplinarian. When he looks up at me with his big hazel eyes, his mother's eyes, I feel all warm and gooey inside; and so I let him go down the slide a couple more times. Finally, after much begging and pleading and possibly even some tears, we head home.

That's when the drudgery begins in earnest. My mother says the hour before Dad got home was always the busiest of her day. Dad would march through the door demanding dinner immediately. Pam doesn't mind and, in fact, prefers to eat after Nicholas has gone to sleep; but still, the hour before she gets home is my most frantic. I sweep and mop, in a state of nervous haste, fearful of Pam's wrath if she comes home and finds the house in a mess. I make Nicholas dinner—leftovers, microwaveable chicken chunks, broccoli, corn, whatever's easy—which we eat while watching the six o'clock news. Sometimes when Pam comes on, Nicholas yells out, "Mommy! Mommy!" and bursts into tears. I have to try to console him. Other times, though, he seems hardly to notice or care.

After she comes home, we have cocktail hour/family fun time, sometimes with the television quacking in the background, babbling, muttering and quarrelling with itself, cracking up at its own jokes. Then Pam puts Nicholas to bed, and I get started on dinner. They haven't seen each other all day, mother and child. They laugh and play and have a great time changing diapers, brushing teeth or having a bath together. I put the baby monitor on and listen to the squeals of joy and happiness and, of course, the tears of shock and dismay, as I chop and mince, making dinner, thinking, most often, it really is something, that mother-child connection. Whenever I tromp, heavy-footed, up the stairs to see what's so funny or what happened, it's like a Vermeer or Michelangelo: *Mother and Child in the Bath*, *Pietà in the Playroom*.

When Pam comes down, we eat. For the first months of Nicholas's life, we might have watched TV while we ate, but that's where I draw the line now. Apart from everything else, to gobble up delicious risotto or rack of lamb while staring at Arnold Schwarzenegger or Steven Seagal engage in crunchy combat with some unlucky villain is an insult to the chef. We eat at the table, have an actual adult conversation, even light some candles. After all, our time on earth is short and getting shorter every day; we should try to live each day to the fullest of our ability and circumstances.

After dinner, if I've been invited anywhere, to Pam's amazement I'll summon reserves of energy I didn't know I had and, even if it's a weeknight, hit the streets. Something about getting dressed up gets me going, I can feel the adrenalin coursing through my veins. "It's showtime!" I'll think, checking myself out in the mirror while rap music pumps out of the ghetto blaster here in my sanctum sanctorum, shaking my big white butt in time to the music.

"You're exactly like a teenager," Pam will say, shaking her head. To which I reply, very seriously, "Pam, whole days go by where I talk to no one except Nicholas. At night I need to talk to people, see some faces, or else I'll go crazy."

I think she understands. She doesn't complain, usually; she knows how I am. If, on the other hand, I haven't been invited anywhere, I'll head out to the porch for a smoke, saying to myself, "Smoking is one of the few pleasures left to the faceless drudge." I only smoke after the sun goes down. This system works well for me. If you have an unbearable craving for a smoke during the day, you can always say to yourself, "I can wait until tonight"; by the time night rolls around, you don't want that many. At most I smoke four or five cigarettes a day. Healthy. And I enjoy them more, I think, than someone who smokes all the time. I experience what 'Nam-haunted writer Thom Jones calls in "The Pugilist at Rest" "the overmastering pleasure that tobacco can bring if you use it seldom and judiciously."

(I have many childless friends, both singles and couples; it's very important to me to maintain my friendships with non-parents, for a number of reasons, one of which is you can usually smoke in their apartments, you don't have to stand outside like a hooker.)

"Don't forget, it's garbage night," Pam might coo to me on my way out, in which case after smoking, I'll wrestle the bags through the garden door and heave them next to our neighbour's garage in the alley behind our house.

In the alley, struck by some nameless urge, the faceless drudge might even lift his head and muse on the moon a bit; then head inside and crash.

12. HOW TO DAD

          I have a book here in my office/dressing room/home gym with that silly title. The book is comprised of thirty-eight one-page chapters, each with an illustration, and even though it was published in 1990, it covers only the fun/recreational aspects of fatherhood: "How to Throw a Spiral," "How to Ride a Bike," "How to Bait a Hook," "How to Shuffle Cards," etc. The only reference to anything drudgery-like is the last chapter, "How to Change a Diaper," and it adopts a strictly jocular tone: "no book of modern dad skills would be complete without instructions for changing a baby's diaper. Fortunately, the near-total extinction of cloth diapers has made the whole process pretty much a no-brainer anyway. . . ."

          Meanwhile, the companion volume, *How to Mom*, doesn't stint on the drudgery-related tips. It has chapters on "How to Pack a Lunch Box," "How to Make Chicken

Soup," "How to Give a Bath," "How to Do the Laundry,"
etc., and the last chapter, "How to Build an Ego," says,
"*only* the unabashed enthusiasm of a devoted mom can
bolster a child's ego."

What about the unabashed enthusiasm of a devoted
dad? It's amazing to me how these sex stereotypes persist.
They're built right into the fabric of the language. I love the
difference between the verbs "to father" and "to mother."
To mother is to nurture, to soothe, to take care of; whereas
to father basically means to contribute 500 million sperm:
"Hey, did you hear? Dave's fathered a child! Now he's got to
get out of town, quick!"

There's no reason a father can't mother a child. Biol-
ogy is not destiny. If I can do it, anyone can. It's only other
people's preconceptions that create all the problems for me.
"You babysit today?" the Korean woman at the vegetable
store down the street always asks me. "Mommy work today?"

"Today and every day," I've told her, if once, a thousand times. "His mother works, and I look after him," I say,
hoping to close the subject. But this particular shopkeeper
is incredibly nosy and persistent. She continues her line of
questioning. Where does she get her chutzpah? I never ask
about her life. What gives her the right to pry into mine?
For a while, I experimented with giving her deliberately
obtuse, enigmatic answers. For example, if she asked, "You
babysit today?" I'd say, "Yes and no," or "I have no answer
to your question." She would smile in a puzzled fashion
and say, "What you mean?" To which I would merely wave
my hand in a deliberately ambiguous gesture. This was a
fun game for a while, but then I got bored of it and now
I buy my vegetables across the street, where they don't
pester me with questions.

Anyway, here are a few more realistic, I like to think, tips on how to dad (not to pontificate; as always I merely pass along what seems to work for me, for what it's worth):

How to Get Some Sleep

"I really respect you for what you do, Dave," people will often say to me, obviously overcompensating for my lack of status in society. "Looking after a kid is the hardest thing in the world to do," they'll sometimes piously add.

It's true that it's more work than an office job; but actually I don't find it all that tough. You can make it tough. But it doesn't have to be. First, you have to face one fact. You're old now. You're ancient! And if you don't believe me, ask a kid how old they think you are. "Fifty-seven?" "Seventy-three?" In the little time that remains to you on this planet, you have to pace yourself. You have to conserve your energy. Of any prospective activity, you must ask yourself, "Approximately how many kilojoules of energy will this cost me?" You have to rope-a-dope your kid, Muhammad Ali's old trick where he hung back against the ropes with his gloves in front of his face and let his opponents punch themselves out.

The most difficult aspect of being a parent, I feel, is the sleep-deprivation aspect. I'm so tired all the time. . . . Man, do I miss those bacheloriffic days, when I might open one eye, see it was "only" eight o'clock, roll over with a groan and go back to sleep. I've felt well-rested maybe four times in the last two years. It's awful. I can't wait until Nicholas is a teenager and starts to sleep in. I try to explain to my childless friends how it feels: "Imagine getting up in the middle of the night, when you're sound asleep," I say, "and having to deal with something for fifteen minutes or half an hour or maybe even an hour or more, then finally going back to sleep, but just as you're drifting off, you're woken up again and you have to go deal with something again. Imagine this going on all night. Then imagine having to get up for good at around six to face your day. Imagine how tired you'd feel. Well, that's how tired you *do* feel! Nothing changes! You don't adapt! You just feel really, really tired all the time."

They just shake their heads, smile and shrug. They don't get it. They understand *intellectually*, but otherwise it's all Greek to them.

"Just you wait," I think maliciously. "Soon enough, Beelzebub willing, you'll know *exactly* what I'm talking about."

But God sends us problems for a reason, I believe, and sometimes I think being tired all the time is good for your spiritual development. Being tired all the time strips away pretension and falsehood. It's like a corrosive acid that burns everything else away to reveal a valuable etching underneath. You have to learn to enjoy life while being tired and worrying about money, I often tell myself; because you will always be tired, and you will always worry about money.

Trying to get Nicholas to sleep was my way into fatherhood, my entry, the low door in the wall (to use Evelyn Waugh's construct) I had to find and go through in order to learn how to dad.

We "Ferberized" Nicholas—we used the techniques described in *Solve Your Child's Sleep Problems* by Dr. Richard Ferber, director of the Center for Pediatric Sleep Disorders at Children's Hospital in Boston. In fact, I think it's safe to say *Solve Your Child's Sleep Problems* is also one of the books that changed my life. Dr. Ferber basically thinks all kids who don't sleep soundly through the night have a specific problem that can be fixed. This book is an extremely practical how-to manual to help your child learn to nap happily and sleep through the night, alone. Dr. Ferber uses an updated version of the old-fashioned notion of letting them cry themselves to sleep. First, you put them into the crib with their transitional object, the beloved item that helps them make the transition from being with you to being alone. Then you leave the room and let them cry, first for five minutes, then ten, then fifteen, then you go in every fifteen minutes after that. Just to assure them you're around. You are not supposed to pick them up or even touch them, and you can only stay in the room for a couple of minutes.

It was brutal, at first. "Occasionally, when you are increasing the time before you respond to your child, he may cry so hard that he actually throws up," Dr. Ferber writes. "If you hear this happen you should go in even though the 'time isn't up' yet. Clean him and change the sheets and pajamas as needed. But do so quickly and matter-of-factly and then leave again. If you reward him for throwing up by staying with him, he will only learn that this is a good way for him to get what he wants. Vomiting does not hurt your child, and you do not have to feel guilty that it happened. This, like the crying, will soon stop."

Luckily, this didn't happen with Nicholas. No, he just stood up in his crib, hot tears streaming down his cheeks, his cries seeming to say, "Mom, Dad, I thought you loved me. I trusted you, and you have abandoned me, betrayed my little tiny heart which beats only for you."

Pam and I would sit on the stairs, staring at our watches, with tears streaming down our cheeks.

"Has it been ten minutes yet?" Pam might ask me.

"Pam, it's only been *three and a half* minutes," I'd say.

It worked though. It might have been the second or third night that he slept without waking; obviously, we slept through the night, too, for the first time in months. It was a miracle! We felt reborn, born again! After a couple of weeks of sleeping through the night, though, Nicholas began to assert his supremacy, and soon we were going into his room again in the middle of the night. After a couple of months of that, we Ferberized him again, and this time it took, sort of. Now he sleeps through most nights.

I apply the lessons I learned from Ferberization to all aspects of parenthood. What these lessons are exactly is difficult to put into words, but it goes something like this: as in all aspects of life, it's important to have a plan, but also be willing to revise this plan as fresh information becomes available. One without the other is useless: if you have no plan, you're sunk, but if you stick too rigidly to your plan, you're sunk, too. *You* have to set the agenda.

Another way to put it is: if at first you don't succeed, maybe you should try, try again, but, on the other hand, sometimes it's better to acknowledge that maybe your plan was a bad one in the first place, and you need to retreat, re-group and rethink. My number one aphorism for parents is: remember, partial success is still success. Sometimes it's important to know when to say *good enough*.

And remember: You're doing your kid an incredible favour by sacrificing so much of your time, energy and money to bring him/her up. My mother is always saying, "You didn't come with an instruction manual, you know," that old cliché, and agonizing over things she might have done differently. Sometimes she will even apologize for specific, seemingly completely inconsequential events, worrying that she didn't handle them differently.

"Don't be ridiculous, Mom," I always say. "You don't need to apologize. In fact, it's quite the opposite. I love my life, you gave it to me, and I'm incredibly grateful. I never think about the details."

It's the same for Nick, I think. He's lucky to be alive (especially after a day with me). The rest is gravy. I may be a Bad Dad, I may be disorganized, lackadaisical, at times even patently bored. But he's obviously happy to be alive, and I love him. In my own horizontal way, I'm doing my best. I try to give him good fatherly advice, like "Only play in little puddles." For the most part, though, he pretty much seems to bring himself up. All I have to do is guide him, stop him from hurting himself and others, and answer his questions—like the one he asked me the other day: "Dad, what's the funniest thing a monster truck ever did?" Anyway, he won't remember a thing about these years. I'll just tell him what a great dad I was (and try to keep this book away from him), and he'll have to believe me.

How to Keep at Least a Couple of Your Friends

There's no doubt that having a kid tends to switch the emphasis in your life from nighttime to daytime. I'm struggling mightily against this tendency, *forcing* myself to go out, to maintain some semblance of a social life against all odds—but it's a losing battle, I can tell. One solution a few of my friends are experimenting with right now is to restore the notion of the *cinq à sept*, a drink from five to seven before going home. I have to give credit for this idea to my friend Andrew Livingston, a former soirée aficionado (party animal) who has recently been blessed with child, E.P. (Eliza Page) Livingston. He is a big supporter of the *cinq à sept* concept, and even goes so far as to make the claim that whereas "when you're in your twenties all the *good stuff* happens in the hours of midnight to two, now the most important hours of the night are between five and seven."

I'm not sure I would take it that far. But I must say that meeting friends after work (them) or a day of being cooped up in the house (me), before fanning out to our various dinner commitments, is refreshing, relaxing and rejuvenating. Once again, our parents had it right. You need a decompression chamber between the stress of work and the stress of home, and a bar is perfect. In a bar, somehow, you take a step back, and you can even smile at (some of) your problems. And you don't drink too much. In *cinq à sept* culture, it's cool to get a little fucked up, but not too fucked up. That's one life lesson I've deeply learned from cooking: just because a little of something is good doesn't mean a lot of it is great. Just because a little garlic makes something tasty doesn't mean a lot will make it delicious. Same with booze. I'm glad this notion has come to me at this time of life, a time when you have to start managing your vices, or risk having to give them up entirely (unthinkable).

How Not to Become Boring

In his otherwise excellent book *I'll Be the Parent, You Be the Kid*, Paul Kropp urges parents to be as dull as possible. Kids "want us dull as dishwater," he writes. "In fact, they *need* us dull as dishwater. . . . When parents become too interesting, we can overwhelm our kids and really interfere with their growing up."

What? With all due respect, I have to disagree. We're all so concerned about our duties these days: our duties at work, our duties at home, our duty to the community. But we also have a duty to ourselves, and to society as a whole *not* to become boring; and it's a duty sadly neglected by many modern parents, it seems to me.

Having a kid is like being in the middle of a massive renovation project, in that it's so overwhelming that your urge is to talk about it. Don't give in to that urge. Even when people ask me point-blank about Nicholas, I usually just say he's fine, he's great—and change the topic. Most people are just asking to be polite. It pays to remember that. They don't want to hear about his latest babblings, gurglings, or potty developments.

Well, obviously here, as elsewhere, you have to read your audience. Bores share two common identifying traits: 1) they don't listen; 2) they're oblivious to body language. You could be squirming in your seat, shifting your weight from cheek to cheek, checking your watch, suppressing yawns, signalling the bartender for the bill, but they just go on and on. But some people—other new parents, for example—want to hear all the gory details, to affirm their own experience, in which case you are permitted to expatiate at length. Even here, though, I would caution that you ascertain that everyone within earshot is also equally interested. A friend of mine, the same Livingston, went away for a weekend recently that turned out to be a forty-eight-hour talkathon on strictly baby-related topics. Natural, since all the couples present were new parents; but still, he describes the experience as "brutal," and came away feeling like some sort of injustice had been done to him, and that some divine restitution is owed him, that he should be given that weekend back, or something.

How to Get Your Kid to Obey You

Pam is always making what is in my opinion the dreadful mistake of asking Nicholas whether he wants something, or wants to do something, or not. Want to put your coat on, Nicholas? Would you like to go to the park, Nick? Want some broccoli? His first instinct is always to say "No!" automatically, then reserve the right to change his mind, which is probably a sensible policy. . . . So even if you ask him if he wants something he likes, he says, "No!"

"Want some chocolate milk, Nicholas?"

"No! I don't need chocolate milk!" Pause. "I want— I want *chocolate milk.*"

He says no to everything he doesn't understand or has never heard of, while simultaneously annexing the word to his vocabulary. So if, say, I were to ask him if he wanted a particle accelerator, he would say, "No! I don't need particle accelerator!" Later, perhaps, he will wonder what exactly a particle accelerator *is.*

As a result, Pam and Nicholas are always getting into a battle of wills. I don't need my coat! Nicholas, please, we have to put on your coat, it's cold out, etc. But you have to choose your battles. I have neither the will nor the energy to fight Nicholas over every little thing. In my opinion, you have to use your wiles, your superior brain-power, to *trick* your kid into doing the right thing, into being civilized. Like a judo master, who uses his opponent's superior size and strength against him, you have to use your children's energy and short attention spans against them. I only give Nicholas a choice between things I secretly want him to do: "Would you like to wear this jacket or that one?" or "You want some peas or some broccoli?" Works like a charm every time. I give him the illusion of choice, or a choice of illusions—which is pretty much all you get in this life, anyway, right?

How to Dress

Wear dark colours. But that's always been true, hasn't it? (Don't get me wrong: in a festive, spring-like mood, I might throw on something in a charcoal grey, or navy blue; but mostly I wear various shades of black.) "Clothes are for keeping you warm and for absorbing wine stains," as some anonymous pundit once said. To which I would like to append a short addendum: "not to mention all sorts of other stains and effluvia too horrible to mention." I remember once when Pam was pregnant with Nicholas, we ran into a woman in a coffee shop who said in her wry, seen-it-all parental way that as soon as she entered the coffee shop, her baby "shat himself to the armpits."

"Shat to the armpits?" I recall thinking at the time. "Wonder what she means by that?" Later I found out. She wasn't kidding; nor was she employing a metaphor or any sort of simile or hyperbole or irony. Let's just say that and move on. It's a great moment in a stay-at-home parent's life when you can return to dry-clean-only wear, but in the early stages, at least, you may find yourself making the concession to cotton or other washable fabrics. Once, when Nicholas was sick with an extremely runny nose, all he wanted to do was cling to me and lie on top of me, and (warning: disgusting parental content approaching) I had to change my shirt twice in three hours, and each time it was literally *wringing wet* with gooey snot.

I used to be a dandy. Even if I wasn't expecting to see a single soul that day, I wore all my best clothes on principle, the principle being "You never know into whom you might bump." I had numerous rules and aphorisms regarding clothing, such as "the colour of your socks should always be *between* the colour of your shoes and the colour of your trousers" and "clothing should become progressively darker the farther it progresses away from your body." In other words, a black shirt with a white suit is a no-no.

As a househusband, though, I wear any old stained, paint-splattered rags. Or so I felt during what I now recognize as a low-self-esteem phase of my househusbanding career. It's an important phase in the new parent's life to start wearing dry-clean-only clothes again; a reclamation of adulthood and decency. It's also important not simply to succumb to practicality and get all daddish and suburban and urban-camperish in your style. It's unnecessary, just as it's unnecessary to buy a huge, bulletproof sport-utility vehicle just because you've had a kid, as so many people do these days (never thinking it's precisely these sport-utilities that are going to fry their children's planet to a crisp, first slowly, then quickly).

"First, decide who you are, and adorn yourself accordingly," as Epictetus advised, and it's great advice. I've always had a tough time with it, though. Standing in front of various three-way mirrors, checking myself out from all angles, I'll often ask myself, "What sort of man am I?" The mirror is no help; nor are the salespeople.

Once again it's Pam to the rescue.

"Pam, I can't decide if I'm a punk or an Edwardian dandy."

"Why do you have to be one or the other?" she responded. "You're both."

Yes! When I got a bit of money recently, I invested it in three suits, which I wear to all evening functions. Say what you like about suits, but generations of thought have gone into every detail, and it shows. In suits, you look about as good as you're going to get. And that's the point, isn't it? I believe I've reached the age where you no longer try to make a statement with your clothes, and just pick the most flattering ones. And it's so easy to slap on a suit. No need to worry about mixing and matching; the top and bottom match. They make life easier. After decades of experimentation, I retreat with relief to traditional male costume for social occasions.

During the day, however, I tend to favour army pants, for a number of reasons. They look kind of macho, plus the cargo pockets are good for carrying diapers, pacifiers and juice bottles. I always carry a cloth—and a knife! Not for protection, though of course I'd use it if I had to, but to cut up the fruit I buy for Nicholas as we stroller along. Then I wipe it on my cloth. A "gentleman" should always carry a cloth anyway, I feel; but with a kid, it's absolutely essential. I also carry a tiny spray bottle full of water, which I find really useful for cleaning my glasses, spritzing Nicholas's face to get off stubborn goo, and also for spritzing my own face when I'm really, really tired.

But obviously, the most difficult accessory for the image-conscious househusband to accommodate into his style is the stroller. As I've already mentioned, I feel naked without a stroller in front of me now—but strollers aren't made for men. The one we got at Pam's baby shower is really short and, I found to my surprise, not adjustable. I have to walk beside ours, pushing it with one hand; or else bend over practically double. To try to remedy this problem, I bought a baby backpack, but I rarely use it.

I shopped around some more and bought a little trailer that looks like a chuckwagon and attaches to my bike. It also turns into a stroller, and when we wheel it in the park, sometimes one of the stay-at-home moms will sidle up and ask where I got it. So you see, I've gone from Bad Dad to a guy stay-at-home moms turn to for advice. True, mostly about gear, but these are still early days.

I live in a neighbourhood of punks, drunks and madmen, and it's surprising how sartorially similar they all are, with their T-shirts and baggy, low-rider jeans. The punks are all attached to some mode of transportation: there are bike punks, skate punks, I've even seen a couple of scooter punks going by on their crazy contraptions. I'm a punk, too, I like to think, with my army pants and dyed, spiked hair. What kind of punk am I? A *stroller punk*, I guess. Admittedly there aren't many of us, yet. I've seen one other, pushing his pram around the neighbourhood with one of his punked-out pals. He's big and fat, like me, but young, nineteen or twenty. I've often thought of approaching him, asking him what's his story, how'd he wind up looking after a kid. But he might take offence—and he looks pretty tough. He looks like he could kick my ass! So we leave each other alone.

How to Dress a Kid

Oh, they wear any old rags; they're just *kids*, after all. I buy everything for Nicholas at Goodwill, where nothing costs over three dollars. Dressing kids is fun, because you can add a touch of whimsy—a really long scarf, a crazy hat— and they can pull it off. Most charming, I think, is when children are dressed like little 1940s adults, and I love dressing Nicholas in workboots and pants with suspenders, and of course pompom hats. Children should only wear hats with pompoms.

How to Shop

Shopping is an art form and like any other art form— writing, sculpture, cooking—takes a lifetime to master. That's the challenge. You have to be impulsive yet not impulsive (Grasshopper). It's a unique blend of planning and serendipity—and you have to have a passion for it (and a shopping trip isn't successful unless you feel sick with guilt afterwards). One day I came off so knowledge-able and informed while talking to the owner of a vintage clothes store (about Big E, a rare type of vintage Levis with a capital *E* on the label, which sells for upwards of five hundred dollars apiece) that another customer asked if I were a collector.

"No," I said, deeply flattered. It occurred to me later that I might be getting too serious about clothes, but you have to be serious about *something*, right? Look at Tyler Brûlé. Men in their thirties, I've heard it said, become ei-ther adventurers or connoisseurs. I'm neither, but if I were to move towards connoisseurship, I think I would like to become a clothing collector. I'd get a huge walk-in closet and really do it right. Is that shallow?

How to Keep House

Obviously I'm the last person on this extremely messy, dusty earth to give advice in this department. I'm a terrible housekeeper, the worst. As a little experiment recently, Pam put pillowcases only on her pillows, not on mine. I slept that way for three weeks, then she asked me, "Doesn't it bother you to sleep on pillows with no cases?" The thing was, I *hadn't noticed*. "Typical man," Pam sighed.

But lately I've been thinking of changing my stripes. I don't want to be a typical anything, and to that end I've been amassing a fair amount of theoretical material on the practice of neatness, which I've boiled down to some basic tenets, which I'll pass along, then move along, for fear of inciting charges of hypocrisy:

1. "A place for everything and everything in its place." This, apparently, is the neatnik's credo, and insofar as I've been able to put it into practice, it seems to work like a charm. At the risk of over-explication, you need to make sure you *do* have a place for everything, and then that you do put those things in their place. If you get both parts of that formula right, it seems, your house will be neat; and they say a neat house takes less work to maintain than a messy one.

2. "Do things as they occur to you." This is a credo of my own coinage, my contribution to the literature, if not the practice, of neatness. One thing that happens when you become a parent is you realize that time is no longer unlimited, a vast amorphous eternity, but composed of minutes and hours. Parenthood effectively eliminates the concept of "later." When you're a parent, later never

comes. Life is a matter of minutes and hours, minutes and hours that are always slipping away; and if you're going to get something done, it's now or never. . . .

3. Get the right tools for the job. I knew I was a true house-husband when I found myself actually getting excited about buying a top-of-the-line mop. Or when Audrey asked me once, offhandedly, but in all seriousness, "Don't you just love chamois?" Of *course* not, I was about to retort indignantly; but then realized that I do, in fact, love chamois very, very much. Not only chamois but dustpans, brooms, vacuum cleaners and all the other tools of the trade, not to mention those not normally associated with keeping house: hammers, paintbrushes, drills, saws, screwdrivers. After all, part of keeping house is to perform minor maintenance chores, something men have always done. If, as the architect Ludwig Mies Van Der Rohe says, a house is "a machine for living," then I stay home and tinker with mine, tune it, keep it oiled, lubricated and running smoothly. Or, to employ a less mechanistic metaphor, like the little prince in Antoine de Saint-Exupéry's charming fable, I clean out my volcano and weed my baobabs. "It is a question of discipline," as the little prince said. "When you've finished your own toilet in the morning, then it is time to attend to the toilet of your planet, just so, with the greatest care. You must see to it that you pull up regularly all the baobabs, at the very first moment when they can be distinguished from the rose-bushes which they resemble so closely in their earliest youth. It is very tedious work, but very easy."

Of course, Antoine de Saint-Exupéry, being childless, couldn't have known about the next principle of house-keeping, which is:

4. Multi-tasking. When you have a toddler, you have to not only do the chores around the house, but amuse your kid as you do them. For example, if I'm making the bed, I have to play hide-and-seek with Nicholas at the same time: "Where's Nicholas? Is he under the pillow [fluff, straighten]? Is he under the sheet [spread, smooth]? Maybe he's under the mattress [tuck, tuck]?" Thus I'm able to get a few minimal chores done. Oh, and a cordless phone's a must, so you can chase him around and/or do dishes while you yak.

How to Travel Light

Despite being a househusband, I am still a man. Every cell in my body contains not only an X but also the smaller, dominant Y chromosome, which carries, among others, the gene for hairy ears and also, although this has yet to be proven scientifically, the gene responsible for the love of packing—that is, packing light. Whenever Pam goes anywhere with Nicholas, she stuffs a huge, bulging bag with diapers, juice, changes of clothes, books, toys and everything else she can think of to cover every possible contingency. I put a diaper in my pocket, and we're off. I like to travel light. We can score some juice and whatever else we need on the road. This is a *city*, after all; all you really need to pack is *money*.

How to Stay Faithful to Your Wife

It may be a minority viewpoint, but I think it's worth mentioning in an age of rampant fatherlessness that to be a good dad, it helps if you're actually around. It's just simpler, and kids like things simple. They're adaptable, of course. They can learn to say, "This is my stepdad's third wife's husband"; but I feel that it's better if they don't have to.

Which means sticking it out in a monogamous relationship—easier said than done, obviously. As I write this, the president of the United States is undergoing a painful and protracted scandal surrounding an extramarital affair he had with a twenty-four-year-old intern. He was hoping to keep it a secret, obviously, but now all the lurid details are coming out. He's learning the truth of Oscar Wilde's observation, which he made after his own trial and scandal, in his long letter from prison, *De Profundis*, that "what one has done in the secret chamber one has some day to cry aloud on the housetops." It's excruciating to watch, but also fascinating, because the entire world is getting a glimpse into something we rarely see: the true, sordid details of an extramarital affair.

Men are simply not hard-wired for monogamy, as I believe everyone understands by now. It's the so-called selfish gene that pushes us to attempt to impregnate as many different women as we can, thus increasing the likelihood of the survival of our DNA unto numerous generations; whereas women are pre-programmed to nurture and to try to keep the father around as long as possible. Hence the battle of the sexes.

And this problem gets worse rather than better as you get older, it seems to me. I know Socrates famously said he was looking forward to old age because it would free him from the tyrannical master of lust, but with all due respect, it seems to me to be quite the opposite: the older men get, the more they're tormented by the desire for young flesh, the more they're willing to throw away on the off chance of getting lucky with a sexy young thing—morals, marriages, mortgages. You can have the respect of the community and the love of your handsome wife, you could win the Nobel Prize, the Whitney could be doing a retrospective of your work, you can be the president of the United States—and an attractive young woman can knock over the entire house of cards with a single manicured nail, can shatter your *Weltanschauung* with a single hair-flip.

What do you do about it? I'm going to give you a piece of advice that may seem disastrous and indeed probably is so: *Overexpose yourself to the source of temptation*. If you find yourself attracted to someone, gentlemen, spend an incredible amount of time with that person, *until you become bored*. So much of sex is about mystery, the unknown; once the mystery dies off, you may find the attraction will too.

I think this advice would have worked for the president of the United States. Imagine if, instead of using his intern, Monica Lewinsky, as a late-night sex-doll, he'd gone out with her for numerous lunches, *cinq à septs*, even long, drawn-out dinners with her in mostly empty Indian restaurants—he might eventually have become bored of her inane chatter, detumesced and ended the affair before it began.

That's the theory, anyway. Obviously, this advice isn't for everyone, only for the strong-willed. And even then I would caution you to be completely sober at all times and meet only in broad daylight, preferably with other people around. Try it, that's all I'm saying—and if it doesn't work, well, contact my solicitors, c/o Random House of Canada, 33 Yonge Street, Suite 210, Toronto, Ontario.

Of course, it helps to marry well in the first place; or, if you're going to marry poorly (as I'm always instructing the young), do it early, so at least you're still youngish when it blows up in your face.

How to Love

Men have to learn how to love, I think, and sometimes it seems to me as if the whole of human history were geared towards teaching men how to love. In *The Family, Sex and Marriage in England, 1500–1800*, for example, Lawrence Stone says that, partially because of high infant mortality rates, "in the sixteenth and early seventeenth century very many fathers seemed to have looked on their infant children with much the same degree of affection which men today bestow on domestic pets, like cats and dogs." He quotes Montaigne, who wrote, "I have lost two or three children in infancy, not without regret, but without great sorrow." As Stone drily notes, "the phrase 'two or three' indicates a degree of indifference and casual concern which would be inconceivable today."

(We've certainly come a long way since then, gentlemen. The other day I was shopping for groceries in the St. Lawrence Market, a huge indoor gourmet market with numerous vendors, and in the middle of it all, Nicholas started to exude a ripe, diaperful odour. "Oh, no. What on earth am I going to do now?" I thought as I half lugged, half pushed his stroller down the stairs to the men's room. What I usually do in these situations, I figured: lay Nicholas out on the cool tile floor of the bathroom and change him while the other washroom patrons flap in and out of the stalls, averting their eyes, and Nicholas stares up at me, blinking and trusting. That was my plan as I pushed him through the door, arms full of bags, beads of sweat starting to form on my face. A lone man was in there, standing against the wall, drilling a late-afternoon leak into the wall. I lay Nicholas down on the none-too-clean floor and looked up and saw what I thought was a mirage. My mind couldn't even process what it was at first: there, bolted to the far wall, was a flip-out change table. In the *men's washroom*. It felt like a miracle, or as close to one as I was going to get.)

I had to learn how to love, too; and I'm still learning. I suppose, on some level, I loved Nicholas from the start, even if my first glimpse of him was a little lunch-loosening. I knew I had to protect this helpless bundle, keep him warm and shield him from harm. But I wasn't quite prepared for the way I feel about him now, now that he's two. Now I think, here is a love which could really break my heart. I'm like a lovesick teenager around him, always making little unrequited passes at him (he's so beautiful). Trying to kiss his neck, smooth out his hair . . .

"No!" he'll sometimes say. "Don't kiss me! Don't pat me!"

"Don't do that, Nicholas," Pam will say. "You're hurting your father's feelings."

And it's true; it stings a bit. But one of the beauties of being a man is it doesn't really hurt that much. I can get over it. I mean, I *care*, but . . . Anyway, I know that later he'll run up to me saying, "Big kiss! Big kiss!" and plant one on my knee. Pam and I are always saying to him, "We love you more than you could know, Nicholas." It's almost like a kind of reflex. What do we mean by that? I sometimes wonder. This love, it's a kind of deep approval. I *approve* of Nicholas more than he could know; I approve of him on a cellular level.

It's monkey love. Having a kid really puts you in touch with your simian roots. Nothing convinces me more that we're all just a bunch of monkeys than the sight of Nicholas tumbling around the couch with a banana in his hand (he's crazy for bananas). It's monkey love, and I'm a love monkey, a love junkie. I'm so used to having him crawl all over me now that it feels funny when he isn't.

I'm glad Pam forced me to have him before I was really ready. Sometimes you have to do things before you're really ready, that's my new motto. True both of living and of dying. Looking back, if it had been up to me, I probably would have had kids, but not until I was forty-four or forty-five. There's nothing wrong with that. You see it all the time these days: guys at the park who you think must be the babies' grandfathers, but they turn out to be the dads. But having a baby demands a certain amount of youthful energy. And now I'm going to need even more of it, because another one's on the way. Yes, Pam's won that battle, too. Although, in truth, I didn't put up too much resistance this time.

"We should make another baby, Dave," Pam kept saying. "We do it so well. . . ."

"Yeah, it's easy for you women," I said, half jokingly. "It's we men who have to look after them."

But how could I argue with her? In the first place, I'm too tired; second, Nicholas is a joy, a ray of sunshine, the angel in the room downstairs, and who am I to deny him a brother or sister? Before you have kids you think of "children" as this abstract concept; afterwards you discover you've brought an individual person, a spirit, a new being into the world— and everything changes. We'll figure something out.

I'm happy. In fact, it's come as something of a surprise to me that family life is capable of providing more sustained happiness than I ever expected to enjoy on this earth. I was going to say "traditional" family life there, but then of course we're not exactly a traditional family, are we? Though it feels that way at times . . . Tolstoy was wrong: all happy families are *not* alike. We're a happy family, just one in which the mother earns the money and the father changes the diapers.

I'm only sorry I have at most thirty or forty years left to enjoy it all. It's going to go by awfully fast. Every year goes by faster, it feels like. Nick is two and a half now. The other day as I was pushing him back from the grocery store, I was trying to explain to him about how time accelerates as you grow older.

"You see, Nicholas, when you're young, time goes slo-o-ow," I said, drawing out the vowel by way of illustration. "But when you get older, time goes by faster and faster." And I sped up the stroller, also by way of illustration.

He amazed me with his response. It was not one of his first two or three fully formed, well-articulated sentences, but certainly among the first two or three dozen.

"No, no, Dad," he said, twisting back to look at me. "Time goes fast for me, too."

"I didn't know that, Nick," I said, talking to him like an adult, as I always do. "But if you say so, I believe you."

He nodded, as if confirming his statement. Then, feeling the need to inject some sort of fatherly wisdom, I said, "I guess the thing is we should try to make the most of whatever time we have."

He nodded again.

EPILOGUE:

PREPARATION

FOR PARENTHOOD

(adapted from the Internet)

Preparation for parenthood isn't just a matter of reading books and decorating the nursery. Here are a few simple tests for expectant parents to take to prepare themselves for the real-life experience of being a mother or father.

1) Walk around the living room from 5 P.M. till 10 P.M. carrying a wet bag weighing approximately eight to twelve pounds. At 10 P.M. put the bag down, set the alarm for midnight and go to sleep. Get up at 12 A.M. and walk around the living room with the bag again, until 1 A.M. Put the bag

down and set alarm for at 3 A.M. As you can't go back to sleep, get up and make a drink. Go to bed at 2:45 A.M. Get up at 3 A.M. again when alarm goes off. Sing songs in the dark til 4 A.M. Put the alarm on for 5 A.M. Get up. Make breakfast. Keep this up for five years. Look cheerful.

2) Can you stand the mess children make? To find out, smear peanut butter onto the sofa and jam onto the curtains. Hide a fish stick behind the stereo and leave it there all summer. Stick your fingers in the flower beds, then rub them on the walls. Cover the stains with crayon.

3) Dressing small children is not as easy as you might think. First buy an octopus and a string bag. Attempt to put the octopus in the string bag so none of the arms hang out. Time allowed for this: all morning.

4) Sell the Miata and buy a minivan. Buy a chocolate ice cream bar and put it in the glove compartment. Leave it there. Stick a quarter in the cassette player. Mash a family-sized bag of cookies down the back seats. Run a garden rake along both sides of the minivan.

5) Get ready to go out. Wait outside toilet half an hour. Go out the front door. Come in again. Go out. Come back in. Go out again. Walk down the front path. Walk back up it again. Walk down it again. Walk very slowly down the road for five minutes. Stop to inspect minutely every cigarette butt, piece of used chewing gum, dirty tissue and dead insect along the way. Retrace your steps. Scream that you've had all you can stand until neighbours come out. Give up on original purpose of walk and go back into house.

6) Take a fully grown goat to the local supermarket. If you intend to have more than one child, take more than one goat. Buy your week's groceries without letting the goats out of your sight. Pay for everything the goats eat or destroy.

7) Hollow out a melon. Suspend it from the ceiling and swing it from side to side. Get a bowl of soggy cereal. Attempt to spoon into hole in melon while pretending to be an airplane. Continue until bowl is half empty. Tip the rest into your lap, making sure a lot of it falls on the floor.

Congratulations! You're ready to be a parent!